Contents

Acknowledgments

In this book I have drawn on a variety of sources. The published sources are recognised in the references that are cited in the text, but the sources also include the intellectual climate created by friends and colleagues and the occasions of teaching and learning that I have been part of with students. There are too many people to mention individually, but a number are members of the International Research Institute for Māori and Indigenous Education at the University of Auckland. Others are staff and colleagues in the School of Education. I have particularly valued the collegial support and critical friendship of Margie Hohepa, Linda Smith, and Graham Smith. Others are colleagues more distant from Auckland who have been prepared to discuss with me issues to do with culture, development, learning, and teaching. I hope my work here appropriately recognises their presence and contributes to their scholarship.

While this is not a book that reports on a specific research project, several recent projects have provided influential settings for the growth of my ideas. These include the intervention programmes in the South Auckland area with Māori and Pacific Islands communities and early childhood and primary teachers. I am indebted to these communities and teachers for the privilege of working with them. Colleagues with whom I have worked and with whom I have learned include Julia Barber, Ana Koloto, Shelley MacDonald, Gwenneth Phillips, Fa'asaulala Tagoilelagi-Leota, Lavinia Turoa, and 'Ema Wolfgramm. The New Zealand Ministry of Education generously funded those studies, and colleagues such as Brian Annan and Corinne Hansell provided valuable advice.

Over the last few years, I have been closely involved in issues to do with national policies in literacy and education. While this book is about children and teachers and the meeting of their minds, I am mindful of how the need to transfer knowledge and have research-based knowledge tested in actual classrooms and conveyed in actual policies has influenced my thinking. My experiences on the Literacy Task Force and the Literacy Experts Group in New Zealand and the close working relationship with Sue Douglas from the Ministry of Education have helped in the writing of this book.

Meeting of Minds

Stuart McNaughton

Learning Media

Cover image by Colin McCahon, entitled *The Days and Nights in the Wilderness; A Constant Flow of Light Falls on the Land*, 1971. Reproduction permission courtesy of the Colin McCahon Research and Publication Trust. Acrylic on unstretched canvas. Auckland Art Gallery Toi o Tāmaki, gift of the McCahon family, 1988.

The author would like to thank the following for their kind permission to reproduce the work credited below.

Figure 1. Reproduced by permission of Oxford University Press, Australia. From *Patterns of Emergent Literacy*, by Stuart McNaughton, 1995, Oxford University Press, www.oup.com.au

Table 1, Figure 3, and Figure 4. Reproduced by permission of the New Zealand Ministry of Education. From Phillips, G., McNaughton, S., and MacDonald, S. (2001). "Picking Up the Pace". *Report to the Ministry of Education*. Wellington: Ministry of Education.

Figure 5. Reproduced by permission of Heinemann. Figure first published in *Stirring the Waters: The Influence of Marie Clay*, edited by Janet S. Gaffney and Billie J. Askew, 1995. Published by Heinemann, a division of Reed Elsevier Inc., Portsmouth, NH, USA.

Published 2002 by Learning Media Limited,
Box 3293, Wellington, New Zealand
www.learningmedia.com

Text copyright © Stuart McNaughton 2002
Design by Sabrina Malcolm

Distributed in the United States of America by
Pacific Learning, P.O. Box 2723
Huntington Beach, CA 92647-0723
www.pacificlearning.com

Printed in China

Dewey number 372.6
ISBN 0 478 24741 9
Item number 24741
PL-9937

The University of Auckland's generous research and study leave provisions have enabled me to complete this book. The funding and support provided by the Woolf Fisher Trust and the University of Auckland in association with Manukau Institute of Technology led to the establishment of the Woolf Fisher Research Centre. The writing of this book has been made possible by having this research base. The administrator of the Woolf Fisher Research Centre, Pauline Te Kare, has been a close colleague since 1998, and my writing owes much to the support and technical skill that she has provided to keep that research centre operating effectively.

I have enjoyed immensely working with both the editor, Michael Keith, and the project manager, Ali Everts, at Learning Media Limited. They have contributed greatly to the crafting. Also, Lois Thompson provided exceptional advice, and her support for the project is much appreciated.

Lastly, I want to thank my family for putting up with me while I have been writing this book. Particularly in the last year, their support, encouragement, forbearance, and love have kept me on track. Thank you, Trudie, Sam, Talia, and Harry. This book is dedicated to you.

Foreword

This is a book that is equally accessible to student teachers and to many stakeholders in education – old hands tired of fruitless debates, boards of trustees, and evaluators of educational outputs, journalists, diverse cultural groups, and international educators who watch the changes New Zealand makes to its education system.

It brings together research analyses that are hot off the press, with a blend of theories that count, including some enduring perspectives from developmental psychology from the last two decades (Au, Bronfenbrenner, Cazden, Delpit, Dyson, Olson and Bruner, Rogoff, Valsiner, Vygotsky, and Wertsch, to name a few) and some very interesting autobiographical reports from several decades ago in the Native School Service of New Zealand.

Most remarkable is the author's treatment of extreme views on several issues. He supports a theory of learning to read and write as complex activities. Therefore, he can argue that teachers must build on to what is already familiar and that they are also responsible for introducing children to what is unfamiliar. And he can insist that 'great expectations, efficacy of teaching, and excellence of outcome' apply to all children, including those from diverse cultural and linguistic backgrounds. Misunderstandings that block effective teaching are shifted in discussion to conceptual solutions that encourage a wider range of more flexible practices in classrooms.

This is a refreshing collection of sane resolutions for a school to immediately apply to its discussions of day-to-day activities in its playgrounds and classrooms! Such material is particularly welcome in an education system that suddenly resolved to 'close the gaps' in educational achievement and just as suddenly found that slogan to be unacceptable. This book's title could be used inclusively to think about children learning from parents and teachers or teachers learning from children and colleagues and used by evaluators, administrators, the public, and politicians searching for ideas about adapting classroom practices for children from different cultural or language backgrounds.

I met Oskar for the first time in the Prologue but have seen him time and again throughout a very long career as a teacher, a therapist, and a researcher. Keep Oskar in your mind as you read this book. A child like him cannot wait until tomorrow; the time for him to develop is, imperatively, today.

This is a readable book about our current need to teach children from diverse language and cultural backgrounds more effectively. Stuart McNaughton leads us into issues that will require a 'meeting of minds' if we are to understand where new practical solutions might be found. He invites teachers to abandon old beliefs like children not being 'ready' for school, and he displaces the intolerable label of 'children at risk' with the notion of schools that put children at risk.

Constructively, the text proposes ways to solve old dilemmas. Is this theoretical discussion? Yes, it has to be. It takes apart things we do not usually question. Then, with a clear view of the pros and cons of each issue, the author constructs new inclusive solutions.

Specific practices are not recommended; there is no committed advocacy of 'this is better than that'. Rather, teachers are encouraged to widen their options, increase their versatility, and find different routes to common outcomes.

What does the author mean? Part of his argument is to make us readers conscious that the questions 'What does it mean to you? What does it mean to me? What does it mean to the child?' call for a meeting of minds if we are to become aware of how differently we see things and begin to reach some common understandings. Yet, in one sense, it is not theoretical, for if it cannot be made to work in practice, it goes nowhere.

As an independent appraiser of the young child's world, Stuart McNaughton accepts that an understanding of the complexity of minds in interaction calls for complex theory and complex solutions. His comments arise from his own research about cultural interactions with diverse ethnicities and from a background in developmental psychology, behavioural analysis, and cognitive development. He focuses his lens of analysis on literacy competencies in the early years of school and recommends a simple but difficult change. We need to hold expectations of excellence in acquiring literacy for all children.

Marie M. Clay, Professor Emeritus,
University of Auckland, New Zealand

Prologue – Getting at the Problem

There is a problem that lies at the heart of teaching. It is what Jerome Bruner described as the central task of effective teaching and learning. It is "… how human beings achieve a meeting of minds, expressed by teachers usually as 'How do I reach the children?' or by children as 'What's she trying to get at?'" (Bruner, 1996, page 45)

The problem illustrated

You can see a powerful example of minds clashing rather than meeting in Volkar Schlondorff's movie *The Tin Drum*. Little Oskar desperately wants to go to school to be like the other children and read and write. He has deliberately stunted his physical growth, but he has two significant attributes to bring to school. He communicates with a drum, using beat and tone and volume. He also shrieks to such effect that he can shatter glass.

His first and only encounter with his teacher is disastrous. Miss Spollenhaurer asks him questions, but she can't understand the drumming that he beats out in response. Oskar, in turn, resents the demands she makes of him to contribute to classroom routines. She tries to stop his drumming by attempting to remove his drum. He drums even louder. Then, as she strikes his drum, he screams and shatters her glasses. She couldn't hear him, and now she can't see him.

The incident is a bizarre exaggeration – part of a metaphor for grand historical and political themes in Germany. Nevertheless, it captures a familiar image – a new entrant and a teacher not on the same wavelength. Each expects different things of the other and acts in other than expected ways. To add to the confusion, Oskar's language is not the language of the teacher.

Four years after a child's entry to school, difficulties in communication between teacher and child can lead to outcomes such as the interactions described below. The teacher here is regarded as excellent by her colleagues. The child is regarded by the teacher as a poor writer. The teacher has introduced an exciting topic to the whole class and has modelled possible vocabulary for writing about it. However, when Miss A comes to see how William is getting on, the interactions begin in this way – as, indeed, she has already predicted that they will.

"What are you going to do for your brainstorming theme, William?" Silence. Five questions and no response later, William finally utters a single word, "Slimy." She responds enthusiastically and asks him to tell her more. Head down, staring at his book, he mumbles, "Slimy night."

"Ooooh, that sounds scary," Miss A says. "Write that down!" At this point another child attracts her attention to ask for help and she moves on. (Glasswell, McNaughton, and Parr, 2001, page 2)

After twenty minutes, William has written four more words. After two weeks of editing and further conferencing, he has erased all four words. In the first session alone, a peer writes fifty-four words.

The problem illustrated here is what happens when a child and their teacher – two participants in the exciting endeavour of acquiring literacy – cannot co-ordinate and pace each other to have the child learning and producing more and more ways of reading and writing effectively. If this problem is not solved in classrooms on a day-to-day, week-by-week basis, it can compound to the point where a child's chances of learning at school are jeopardised. The solution, according to Bruner, lies in bringing the minds of teachers and learners together.

Part One

Introduction

Chapter 1

Setting the Scene for a Meeting of Minds

Overview of the chapter

What this book is about

This book is about teaching literacy effectively with children of culturally and linguistically diverse backgrounds who are beginning school. These are children who are not from those communities that define the majority culture, often called the "mainstream". Their home language is often not that of the majority. They are, in certain respects, children for whom going to school is a risky business, children for whom the early "meeting of minds" between teacher and learner can make all the difference between success and failure in acquiring literacy at school. They are children who often feature more prominently in the problems that can arise from these minds not meeting. When such problems become associated with one group rather than another, they take on a political as well as a social significance.

This book looks at meeting the needs of children from diverse backgrounds in standard classrooms in mainstream schools by the deliberate enhancement of literacy instruction. It is not the first book to examine what makes literacy instruction effective for such children. Much has been researched and written, and in the following chapters, we will survey this literature, sometimes questioning and sometimes adding to what is understood.

A note on evidence from research

The evidence used in this book for what constitutes effectiveness in teaching and learning comes from several sources of research. It is complicated, as is often the case when research based on how teaching and learning occur in the actual classroom is used. There are four main sources:

- descriptions of a strategy in action, with some evidence provided by transcripts or other descriptions of children's engagement in instruction;
- case study descriptions of effective teachers;
- experimental tests of effective practice undertaken in real classrooms (which can show outcomes both from a moment-by-moment engagement with instruction and from longer-term progress and achievement);
- basic (often laboratory-based) experimental studies of learning and teaching that usually provide specific outcomes on controlled tasks.

None of these sources is sufficient on its own to establish the effectiveness of a particular strategy, approach, or set of conditions. But if some support comes from them all, then a credible case for effectiveness can be made.

The widening gap in literacy

In New Zealand, literacy instruction is commonly regarded as very effective, and clearly it is, at least by international standards.[1] However, there are groups of students who make relatively low levels of progress in developing literacy. They are mainly indigenous Māori children and children from Pacific Islands immigrant families, particularly those in schools serving communities with the country's highest unemployment and lowest income levels.

At entry to school, when the literacy and language skills usually associated with success in schools are measured, there are already differences between these groups of children and other groups.[2] Some differences, such as in recognising letters and knowledge of letter and sound relationships, reduce. Others, such as in word knowledge, writing vocabulary, and text reading level, develop and increase over the first year.

The differences become even more noticeable after four years. Substantial differences have developed in reading, particularly in comprehension of different types of texts, and in writing. Similar patterns of difference occur in other countries.[3] The widening gap in the measures of literacy parallels the gap existing between the minds of these learners and their teachers.

Making a difference to children "at risk"

The meeting of minds is a problem that faces all teachers with all children. However, the problem is particularly significant in schools serving communities with cultural and language identities different from those of the majority culture. It is on the classrooms in such schools that this book focuses. Their communities include indigenous groups, long-term "involuntary minorities" (Ogbu, 1991), and recent immigrant groups.

All of these often have less access to social, economic, and political power than those from mainstream communities.

Children from these communities face special difficulties in the classroom and as a group are "at risk" of not achieving the same levels of literacy as other groups. This will, in turn, impact on their future employment, income levels, and other ways of accessing economic and social resources. However, there are three sorts of evidence that the difficulties are not inevitable.

Effective teachers

The first sort of evidence comes from the classroom. Effective teachers can make a difference. Contemporary meta-analyses* of classroom innovations show that substantial effects on student achievement can be produced by such innovations. Furthermore, individual studies identify the characteristics of the teachers involved. This is not new – the history of schooling contains compelling examples of effective teachers and schools in New Zealand's colonial past and in early schooling in the United States for African American children.[4]

Alternative kinds of schools

The second sort of evidence comes from radical alternatives to standard schooling. For example, an alternative exists in New Zealand in the form of indigenous Māori schools (Kura Kaupapa Māori). These schools are cultural institutions designed to regenerate a language at risk and to amplify cultural practices, as well as to deliver excellent contemporary education. The evidence is that such schools can make a difference. In some areas of the national curriculum, they can offer education that, in effectiveness, matches that available in mainstream schools as well as fulfilling the prerogative to act as a cultural storehouse (Flockton and Crooks, 2000).

New horizons

The third sort of evidence comes from a phenomenon described by Jim Cummins (1986). It concerns students from communities that, in their countries of origin, have historically not been served well by their schools.

---

* Meta-analyses are careful reviews of research evidence from multiple studies.

When families from these communities change countries, they can also experience a dramatic shift in their schooling options. In some cases, this shift is associated with a change in the educational achievement profile of children from the community.

The reasons why this phenomenon makes a difference are various. They have to do with such factors as a shift in social status in the new country, a shift in the nature of the relationship that families have with schools in their new country, and a shift in a perception of control – from being an involuntary minority in their country of origin, the community becomes a voluntary minority in a new country.

The solution – in the ordinary classroom

The option of a radical alternative school is available to only a few children. For example, with regards to the Māori cultural alternative mentioned previously, in 1999, eighty-five percent of Māori students were in standard English-medium classrooms in New Zealand (Literacy Experts Group, 1999).

This means that the issue of delivering effective literacy instruction exists for all teachers with students from diverse backgrounds, and that it will remain compelling, not only for minority indigenous populations, but for some new immigrant groups too. That is why this book is about solving the problem in ordinary classrooms, not in those of alternative schools.

Risky places for promising children

Above, in describing the learners whom this book concerns, the term "at risk" was used. It is not uncommon to use this term when referring to such children. But the notion of being at risk can be viewed in two distinct ways.

At risk because of children's "deficiency"

One way is to see the children and their families as generally "at risk" because they are deficient. The children from these families have less compared with average achievers in their schools. The difficulties they have with their learning arise from, for example, a *lack* of background knowledge or *delayed* language development.[5] The problem of low levels of progress and low achievement is located with them. They, in themselves, constitute a problem to be solved.

The risky business of school

The other way to view "at risk" is to see the children and their families as being at risk in the standard classroom. For them, going to school is a risky business. Their difficulties are located in the teaching and learning that goes on in classrooms. This view assumes that these children come from families that have their own rich processes of learning and development and socialisation. Children whose first language is not English may have limited skills in English, but they may very well have well-developed language and literacy skills in their first (and other) languages. They arrive at school with expertise in the language and literacy practices of their own communities. These may or may not overlap with the expertise recognised by conventional schooling, and this is one reason why classrooms may be risky for them.

Children "with promise"

Anne Haas Dyson (1999b) reframes the view of children from diverse culture and language backgrounds from one of being "at risk" to one of providing teachers with rich cultural resources on which to build. This is echoed by Debra Skinner and her colleagues (1998), who recast the term into one that sees such children as being "with promise".

This is the view of children and their families adopted in this book. However, the notion of risk has been retained because, without a deliberate teaching focus for these children and their families, classrooms will continue to be risky places for them.

Where the minds are "at"
Where are the children at?

The Bruner quote in the prologue highlights a major assumption running through the general theories that we hold about how children learn and how they are taught. This is that effective teaching is somehow determined by the relationship between an act of teaching and the identity of the student – what could be called the "at" principle. In the common wisdom of teaching, this is enshrined in the dictum "start where the learner is at". In other words, we recognise and build on current knowledge and skills.

The focus of this book is on beginning literacy instruction but, even when it is limited in this way, the business of identifying "where the child is at" turns out to be very complicated. What exactly should we identify, and what might we do to build on it? The complexity of any answers to these questions can be illustrated from work on emergent literacy over the last decades (McNaughton, 1995).

Children go to school already knowing and using written language in their daily life, and their expertise ranges from just beginning to markedly competent. This variation in expertise reflects, within and across all communities, the diversity of ways in which written language is used and in which learning and teaching happens in a child's social environment. So every child arrives at school with an individual profile of knowledge and skills. Defining this profile can include markers such as alphabet knowledge or concepts about how books work – the conventional assessment of school literacy. It could also include markers from family and community uses of literacy, such as recitation in church.

For the teacher, knowing where an individual child is "at" is complicated. Knowing where a class of thirty or so children might be at, especially in the beginning stages of formal literacy instruction, is a daunting task indeed. On the positive side, this complexity also means that possible solutions to the problem become more obvious. The outset of formal school instruction – the time when teachers and learners come together for the first time – is a period of developmental transition, when the processes of teaching and learning are thrown into sharp relief.

What's the teacher trying to get at?

The Bruner quote highlights the flip side of the "at" principle – where is the *teacher* at? For a child in the classroom, this is the business of figuring out some serious questions: what are you meant to do, why are you meant to do it, how do you learn to do it better, and how do you learn from what the teacher does? If the child is not used to the words or the ways of the teacher, none of these questions might have obvious or easy answers. Moreover, if the child gets the answers wrong and then continues to get them wrong, the meeting of minds becomes increasingly difficult. The likelihood of their meeting in a way that produces effective teaching and learning becomes correspondingly doubtful.

This is at the heart of the risky business of the classroom, and the reason for this particular risk, elaborated in the following chapters, is the dynamic relationship between teacher and learner. Together, they make up a system of teaching and learning. That is, what a teacher does is a part of what a learner does, which in turn is part of what a teacher does, and so on. Their mutual influence alters each other's ideas and actions immediately as well as subsequently.

When neither teacher nor learner can figure out where the other is at, the dynamics of the relationship can produce strongly negative effects. Studies of how learners make slow progress have uncovered various ways in which both teachers and learners contribute to the situation. Unless one deliberately modifies the system, it is almost as though both teacher and learner, perhaps like Ms A and William in the prologue, conspire to join in a downward spiral of more and more limited teaching and learning. The process is an example of what have been called the "Matthew effects"*.

Continuity – an approach to effective meetings of minds

How do we tackle the problem of the effective meeting of minds? How can we promote such meetings in the face of cultural and language diversity in classrooms? One approach has dominated recent discussion. It concerns continuity – the matching of expertise that children have in their everyday activities outside school with the sorts of entry skills that they need to engage effectively in classroom activities.

The core assumption of the continuity approach is that teaching and learning at school can be made more effective by enhancing the continuity between how things are done at school and how things are done in the child's family and social setting. Various criticisms are made of this approach, but here we assume that creating continuity has an important part to play in making the meeting of minds possible. In the course of this book we identify some of the processes involved in creating continuity – building on the familiar – in order to see how they can contribute to effective literacy instruction.

* From the saying by Jesus in the Gospel according to Matthew: "For those who have will be given more. Those who do not have, even what they have will be taken away from them." (Matthew, 25:29, *The Holy Bible*, New International Version)

Continuity and cultural capital

For some families and communities, there is already a high degree of this kind of continuity with schooling in place. In these, as it were, "spontaneously" well-matched families and schools, the knowledge and activities that are habitually part of home life are already relatively well tuned to those activities at school; or, if you like, the school is well tuned to the activities of the home.

This is the meaning behind the idea of "cultural capital" – the term contemporary sociology uses for the storehouse of experiences, knowledge, and attitudes a child can capitalise on when going to school, given the practices of schooling (Nash, 1993). It is cultural capital that underlies the relationship between achievement in reading and parents' occupational status or income level.

But to call the match between such families and schools "spontaneous" does not mean that it is "natural" or even "appropriate" – terms that would imply that this particular storehouse was somehow better than others. It does mean that some families have in their home and community life certain customs and cultural concepts that provide their children with an effective basis for conventional schooling.

The same set of circumstances, but with a different storehouse, may arise with indigenous forms of schooling such as the previously mentioned Kura Kaupapa Māori. In this case, for example, the cultural capital that families bring to the schools includes aspects of oral Māori language and familiarity with cultural customs and concepts. Families steeped in these are likely to have children who are high achievers in the educational activities of that kind of school.[6]

The continuity approach assumes that the ordinary classroom teaching provided in mainstream schools for children from groups such as Māori does not match well with their culturally based ways of teaching and learning and practices of literacy. Several researchers (Cazden, 1988; Tharp and Gallimore, 1988) argue that if classroom instruction were adjusted to better match how teaching and learning and literacy happened outside school, then children's achievement would be enhanced. The corollary of the argument is, of course, that continuity would also be enhanced if family practices were adjusted to match those of school.

Enhancing continuity

Continuity between families, their community and schools can be deliberately enhanced in three general ways:

- outside school – to modify, adapt, or supplement family, community, and early childhood activities so that literacy practices better match those of the school;
- at school – to modify, adapt, or supplement classroom activities so that they better match those of family, community, or early childhood settings;
- a combination of both.

Enhancing continuity at school

In this book, we will concentrate on examining the deliberate enhancement of continuity through the literacy instruction that happens at school. This is not to undervalue augmenting literacy practices in family and community settings. Nor is it to ignore the superiority of a combined approach, the third way, when teaching children with diverse languages and from diverse cultures. Collaboration between schools and such families and communities is a vital strategy in the continuity approach, particularly when it makes professional knowledge available to families and communities and when family practices are added to rather than undermined (McNaughton, 1995). However, full consideration of these ways of enhancing instruction would require treatment in a separate book.

Critiques of the continuity approach

The continuity approach does have limitations. One is that it has not fully explained the processes that actually contribute to continuity between home and school. What is it that enables students and teachers to make connections between in-school and out-of-school knowledge and skills? Moreover, discontinuities in language practices exist for *all* children, and continuity explanations have not untangled the discontinuities that are common to all children from those specifically facing children with diverse cultural and language backgrounds.[7]

How literacy happens – the socialisation model

To answer these limitations, and also to identify effective literacy instruction, this book employs a framework of ideas on how literacy happens – the socialisation model of literacy development (see Figure 1). The model is based on the view that learning and development are co-constructed in a community's practices (Rogoff, 1990; Valsiner, 1988). Children construct ways of acting with significant family and community members, who function as socialisation agents – they provide a means for children's learning through their interactions with children and through the activities they employ for these interactions. A child's ways of constructing and their family's patterns of guidance are mutually composed, hence the term co-construction (Valsiner, 1988).

At the core of the model – activities

In the model, socialisation is seen as an active process – active in the way in which activities are selected, arranged, and deployed and active in the way in which joint and personal constructions take place within activities. In family settings, a family's social and cultural practices are the source of these activities.

Activities are at the core of the model, and they provide the model's primary unit of analysis. Activities are structured events. Activities have goals, and the participants' actions within the activities are directed towards these goals. There are known patterns of action within activities, but they allow for dynamic variations in participation. A basic assumption about the nature of activities is that if activities are to be the means for learning and development, the participants must come to have shared understandings about the goals of, and ways of acting in, these activities.

Literacy activities – at home

Family literacy activities – reading stories with a child, reading the Bible to a child*, singing an alphabet song, providing materials for children to draw and write, and storytelling – are a subset of these socialisation activities. Like all other activities, they occur in three forms – joint, personal, and ambient. The latter are those that go on around the child, in which they may be peripherally involved as an observer. Each of these

* Bible reading is a familiar activity in the homes of many Pacific Islands families.

forms of activities provides a means for learning and development to take place. The processes by which this happens have been described using concepts such as scaffolding (Wood, 1998) and guided participation (Rogoff, 1990). The processes enable the expertise required to participate in and perform activities to develop while engaging in those activities.

The socialisation model at school

We can see the same sorts of patterns and processes occurring in schools, which act as secondary sites of socialisation. Teachers select, arrange, and deploy particular activities that reflect the socialisation practices of the school. Development and learning take place in joint, personal, and ambient activities. Classroom-based expertise is situated in these activities. The professional roles of the teachers (the agents) and their use of particular tools, such as curriculum documents and resources, set constraints and conditions for what children learn and what develops.

Figure 1

A socialisation model of emergent literacy.

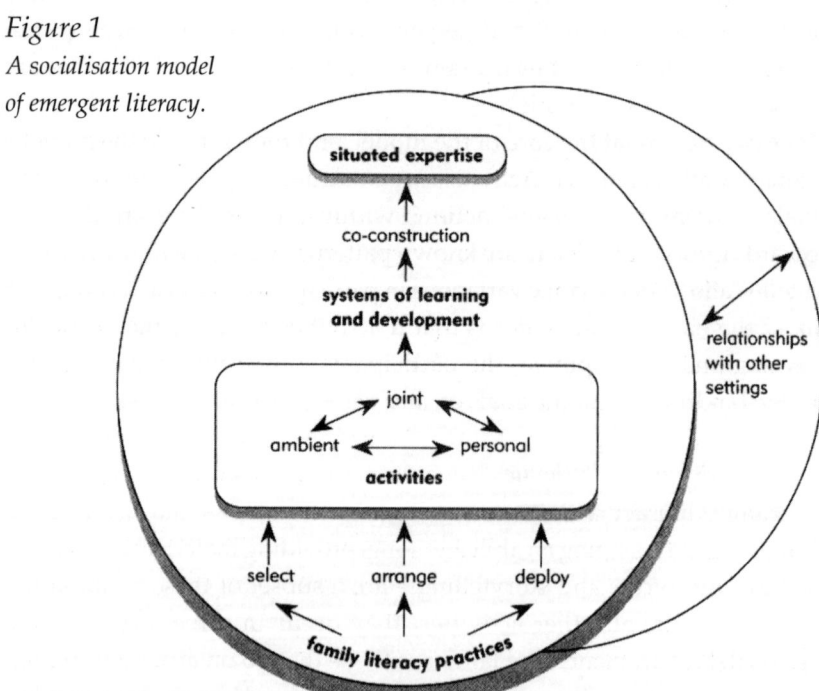

Reproduced by permission of Oxford University Press Australia, from Patterns of Emergent Literacy, *by Stuart McNaughton.*

In this model, expertise develops within particular activities and, at least initially, is situated within these activities, so, before school, children's expertise is developing within familiar activities. When children go to school, they are confronted with new, or at least more intensively patterned, developmental tasks. The curriculum and classroom practices require certain forms of expertise, at certain times, and in certain sequences. To add to the complexity, the ways in which children and their significant adults are expected to participate in classroom activities are in settings of crowded environments where the participants have defined roles as "teacher" and "learner" (Cazden, 1988).

In many respects, the literacy tasks used in classrooms reinforce and complement each other, reflecting the overall goals and values of contemporary schooling. Despite the presence of different instructional approaches, literacy and language events share commonalities across many types of schools. Consequently, children's expertise in literacy and language shifts on a relatively broad front (between the ages of five and seven years), reflecting the range and intensity of developmental requirements in this secondary socialisation site.

Resource-full sites for acquiring literacy

The model depicts family, community, and educational sites for children's learning and development in which the activities that are selected, arranged, and deployed provide guidance for learning, directly or indirectly. Each site can be seen as resource-full – each has resources that are used in guiding language and literacy. Not all families may be able to capitalise on these resources because of difficulties they confront, such as economic hardship or not having access to the knowledge and skills associated with mainstream schooling (Hart and Risley, 1995). But, armed with this model, one can ask questions about the nature and effectiveness of the available resources and the nature of the constraints on those resources.

The multiple ways into literacy

In the model for how literacy develops that we have adopted in this book, it is evident that there are a multitude of sites for the development of literacy. The diversity comes from the processes of co-construction.

Children construct ways of using written language within the various patterns of socialisation that they experience. Multiple forms of literacy with different developmental properties are possible before school. Conversely, it should be possible to capitalise on these forms by using different patterns of guidance and, through different pathways, to achieve the same school literacy outcomes (Clay, 1998; McNaughton, 1995).

This view of the multiple pathways to literacy is very different from the unitary view – that where a learner is at, and where a teacher needs to be at, are points to be located in a single, predetermined, sequence of literacy development – a view that is not supported by the evidence. Take learning to read and write at school. Children learn to read and write under different curricular prescriptions and with different programmes – but they still get to read and write. Similarly, children's development before school comes about from the experience of hugely diverse forms of knowledge and strategies (Elster, 1994; Phillips, Norris, and Mason, 1996), and there is evidence that the various components of reading and writing at school can have many different developmental pathways leading to them.[8]

The challenge of diversity at the start of school

Different forms of literacy knowledge and expertise can develop before school and provide multiple routes to learning at school. The challenge to teachers is one of developing effective forms of mediation, leading Marie Clay to argue that "a starting programme should be so designed that it provides for engagement of different children in different ways on different levels from the beginning" (Clay, 1991, page 203).[9]

Making connections

Armed with this framework of ideas about how literacy happens, we can view the meeting of minds as a matter of enhancing the multitude of sites that learners and teachers have available to them in which to make connections. These connections might be enhanced by building on the familiar – a kind of transfer of learning, as expertise and activities found in one setting are incorporated into another. This is a reformulation of the continuity approach. But they might be enhanced also by unlocking the unfamiliar – a kind of discrimination learning in which awareness of the goals and rules of different activities develops, enabling the boundaries or applicability of different forms of expertise to be discerned. This second approach helps to overcome the limitations of the continuity approach.

Making connections by building on the familiar

From the point of view of the learner, making connections can be understood as a kind of transfer. Effective connections for the learner happen when the activities in an (often unfamiliar) instructional programme incorporate features of some familiar expertise that up until then have been situated in out-of-school activities. Transfer of learning occurs as a consequence of this incorporation* – bridges between the familiar and the unfamiliar can be made both by the learner and by the teacher. Children are better able to engage, and to continue to engage, in classroom instruction (and hence learn from classroom instruction) because they have entry skills – expertise that is immediately functional for the activity. This is like saying that I could get more from a coaching session in tennis if I already knew something about racquet games and could use my previous experience, and if the coach knew that I knew and could incorporate what I knew and what I could do into the session.

This, by the way, is not the traditional psychological account of transfer, which focuses on the learner's knowledge and strategies as though these are independent of any given situation.[10] For the process we are discussing here, the following reconceptualisation of transfer (Bransford and Schwartz, 1999) is useful because it puts the focus on a learner's "preparation for future learning", a focus that emphasises the relationship that existing learning might have with new learning and teaching contexts. In addition, much of what is learned is context specific, and transfer needs to be seen as an issue to do with the relationships between contexts. Thus, the perspective that we have on transfer here is that this "preparation for future learning" is a product of the learner and their settings, including the guidance provided in those settings. A redefinition that incorporates this sense is provided by Dyson, who claims that transfer:

---

* The term "incorporation" is used throughout this book to mean "the process of building on the familiar".

… involves negotiation between and among teachers and learners, as frames of reference for judging "relevant" material are themselves differentiated and expanded. (Dyson, 1999a, page 142)

There is another dimension to the idea of transfer that is important for children of diverse cultural and language backgrounds at school. That is the transfer of a feeling of being "at home" – being comfortable or being affirmed or being recognised. This is a fundamental psychological matter of identity and location. "Do I feel I belong here, and am I at (or could this come to be) my place?" This kind of concern for identification leads writers such as Gloria Ladson-Billings (1994) to argue that a major criterion for the effectiveness of instruction is that it maintains or enhances positive cultural identity. Katherine Au (1993) sees the teacher who incorporates cultural ways in classroom instruction as having the role of a cultural mediator, helping students to feel comfortable with their own identities. Her argument is that enabling students to have their identities affirmed and developed can be done in ways that do not conflict with high literacy achievement.

Making connections through unlocking the unfamiliar

For the learner, making connections might be enhanced further by a kind of discrimination learning – one that is complementary to the process of transfer. Transfer of learning, we have argued, depends on the bridges that are made between the learner's existing activities, knowledge, and expertise and the activities, knowledge, and expertise that are of high educational value. But incorporating out-of-school knowledge and expertise in itself might not guarantee learning those literacy and language uses that are at the core of school curricula – uses that can be markedly different from out-of-school ones in purposes, participation structures, and rules (Hemphill and Snow, 1996).

The idea of discrimination here is that it is a process by which children can come to be aware of how their out-of-school knowledge and expertise are aligned with the instructional activities that they experience at school. There is a general argument in psychology that increasing an awareness of one's acts enhances one's ability to perform them. Similarly, and especially for the unfamiliar learner, an awareness of goals, rules, and ways of performing can enhance effective learning, leading to the learner's greater self-control over performing and decreasing their reliance on external regulation (Clay, 1999).

The example of recitation

For learners, therefore, discriminating between familiar ways of acting and the requirements of new classroom activities should enhance their understanding of both the familiar and the unfamiliar. Take, for example, the recitation of texts that some groups, such as Pacific Islands children, have considerable experience of outside school. Recitation can provide a basis both for the transfer of skills and for the discrimination of appropriateness. In the transfer of skills, for example, recitation can be used to learn text in classroom activities that include the development of decoding skills. A child could draw on their memory skills, honed by recitation, to learn the frame in a simple text such as "Here is the dog. Here is the cat." Recitation skills incorporated into the activity can aid the learner's attending to relationships between what is said (part-memorised) and what is seen.

A reliance on recitation, however, may interfere with the development of other reading processes – ultimately, reading for meaning. This possible conflict raises the need for the discrimination of appropriateness – to bring into play strategies for identifying ideas, making inferences, and evaluating, which the teacher can utilise to enable children to be aware of these particular requirements. In this case, complementing the transfer of a set of skills with guidance on how to be discriminating about applying them adds to the capabilities of learning and of teaching.

Developing awareness for effective teaching and learning

This view of how transfer and discrimination in learning can work together leads to a new perspective on what makes for effective teaching of children from diverse cultural and language backgrounds. It is the need for children to become aware of the fabric of classroom activities so that they understand the goals and rules of these activities and what is required to perform them. Various researchers, whose work we will describe in later chapters, argue that both apprenticeship processes – that is, acquiring knowledge and expertise through immersion in activities – and explicit instruction are required for this to happen.[11] Through such a combination, children not only achieve their learning but also become aware of the ways in which in-school and out-of-school forms of expertise are aligned. The result is a more dynamic form of making connections, ultimately mediated by the learner, the outcome of which is that learners are able to understand and reflect on new forms of expertise.

Lowry Hemphill and Catherine Snow conclude from their analysis of the discontinuities between home and school language practices that simply increasing continuities could easily confuse children. But, because children are problem solvers, and because guidance can be active, a solution is possible.

> *If we view children as skilled linguistic problem solvers, as form masterers, and as flexible sociolinguists, what view of literacy acquisition might we adopt? First, we would expose children to a wide range of spoken and written language genres, involving children in producing as many different varieties of spoken and written language as possible. Second, we would provide activities to develop children's capacities consciously to analyze those genres and how they differ, acknowledging that children can treat language as an object of contemplation, not just as a tool for communication. Third, we would recognise that the rules for producing extended discourse are arbitrary, language-specific, community-specific, and situation-specific, and we would abandon the notion that some forms are natural, universal, and directly accessible.* (Hemphill and Snow, 1996, page 198)

The development of this awareness has a further significance. It enables teachers and children to develop critical literacy with greater power to reflect on social inequalities (Au, 1993). One of the limitations of the continuity approach, according to Bartolome (1998), has been a restricted appreciation of how classrooms can reflect wider inequalities of status. Some cultural groups' ways of using language may not be viewed and treated as legitimate in the classroom, reflecting (and helping to recreate) a "minority" status.

Each knowing where the other is at

The ideas about the processes of transfer and discrimination developed here represent the two sides of the core issue in teaching that Bruner identifies. For the teacher, it is to find where the learner is at, and the idea of transfer is to teach in a manner that enables the learner to bring their ways of learning and their knowledge of and ways with words into the classroom activities. For the learner, it is to understand what the teacher's ideas are and what the classroom actually requires.

Diversity as a strength for effective instruction

In 1997, Linda Darling-Hammond proposed a "blueprint for creating schools that work" based on her summary of a large body of research on schools that were effective in their response to the challenges of schooling in contemporary American society. The two basic planks of her blueprint are:

- To *teach for understanding*. That is, to teach all students, not just a few, to understand ideas deeply and to perform proficiently.
- To *teach for diversity*. That is, to teach in ways that help different kinds of learners to find productive paths to knowledge as they also learn to live constructively together. (Darling-Hammond, 1997, page 5)

This, she argues, will require a major change in education policy, needing efforts that range from designing instruction to developing schools' capacity to take responsibility for student learning and, at the same time, to be responsive to student and community needs and concerns.

The challenge for schools is to see the task of making connections not as one of getting rid of the diversity that they encounter in the make-up of their populations, nor of dealing with diversity as something that has to be coped with, but rather as one of incorporating diversity to the advantage of effective pedagogy. How to do this, at least in the context of early literacy instruction, is the subject of this book.

Overview of the rest of this book

In Part Two, we examine in detail the approach to making connections through incorporation – the process of building on the familiar. In Part Three, our examination shifts to making connections through developing awareness – the process of unlocking the unfamiliar. In each part, the emphasis is on how classroom instruction can enable a meeting of minds to occur and what this entails for teachers. In Part Four, we discuss some other features of classrooms that contribute to effective teaching and learning, notably the role of expectations and the sense of efficacy in both teachers and learners.

End Notes

1   See Elley (1999).

2   See Gilmore (1999).

3   For New Zealand, see Clay (1986), McNaughton (1995), McNaughton, Phillips, and MacDonald (2000), Flockton and Crooks (1997), Wagemaker (1992) and Wilkinson (1998); for other countries, see Darling-Hammond (1997).

4   Hattie (1999) reports on classroom innovations; Ladson-Billings (1994) and Wilkinson and Townsend (2000) report on the characteristics of effective teachers. For historical examples of effective teachers, see Foster (1995) (USA) and Simon and Smith (2001) (New Zealand).

5   For example, Kame'enui and Carnine (1998) state that they wrote their book *Effective Teaching Strategies That Accommodate Diverse Learners* for children of poverty, children with limited English-speaking skills, and children with disabilities.

6   The developmental properties of this idea are contained in Urie Bronfenbrenner's ecological model of human development. He claimed that "The developmental potential of a child rearing setting is increased as a function of the number of supportive links between that setting and other contexts involving the child or persons responsible for his or her care. Such interconnections may take the form of shared activities, two-way communication, and information provided in each setting about the others." (Bronfenbrenner, 1979, page 847)

7   These criticisms can be found in Bartolome (1998), Hemphill and Snow (1996), Losey (1995) and Wood (1998). The criticisms are dealt with in the chapters that detail a complementary approach aimed at developing awareness.

8   See Snow, Barnes, Chandler, Goodman, and Hemphill (1991) and Whitehurst and Lonigan (1998).

9   The discovery of multiple pathways to common developmental outcomes is not limited to language or literacy. It is present in such disparate areas of human development as sensorimotor development in infancy (Thelen, 1995) and in the development of close relationships across the age span (Rothbaum, Pott, Azuma, Miyake, and Weisz, 2000).

10   If one approached the issue as a traditional problem of transfer or generalisation, there would be little cause to be positive and even fewer indications of how to proceed to increase the probability of incorporation occurring. There is precious little demonstration of direct transfer from one task setting to another unprompted task setting (Bransford and Schwartz, 1999; Detterman and Sternberg, 1993). And there is a curious mismatch here between the laboratory pursuit of a phenomenon and everyday educational contexts in which the phenomenon might be promoted. The traditional approach to locating or identifying transfer requires a demonstration in the absence of instruction and prompts. Indeed, a recent review of the literature referred to the methodological problem of subtle "tricks" by experimenters to cue subjects to transfer their learning (Detterman and Sternberg, 1993).

11   See Bartolome (1998), Gee (1998), and Hemphill and Snow (1996).

Part Two

PART 2

Making Connections by Building on the Familiar

Part 2

Making Connections by Building on the Familiar

In the next four chapters, we focus on the part that building on the familiar can play in effective literacy instruction for children from diverse cultural and language backgrounds. We examine how teachers and learners can make connections by incorporating the skills in literacy and language that come from the children's family and community experiences.

But a qualification is needed before we do so. The kinds of strategies, activities in classrooms, and curricula that we discuss here do not provide a description of a full classroom programme or of the characteristics of effective teaching in such a classroom. The analysis presented here involves just one dimension of effective teaching and learning for children with diverse language and cultural identities – that of making connections.

In Chapter 2, *The Meeting Ground – Curriculum and Classroom Activities*, we examine the classroom conditions that promote this kind of incorporation – a space in which a "wide" curriculum operates and where, within that curriculum, versatile activities can be employed.

In Chapter 3, *Strategies for Incorporating the Familiar*, we identify the instructional approaches employed by teachers for making connections and review evidence for their effectiveness.

In Chapter 4, *Getting a Balance – Incorporation and Phonics*, we look at how strategies for incorporation can apply in one specific component of literacy instruction – teaching phonics.

In Chapter 5, *Being an Expert*, we examine the kind of professional expertise – in particular, the awareness of diversity – that a teacher needs in order to capitalise on the classroom conditions and instructional approaches available to make connections with learners.

Chapter 2

The Meeting Ground –
Curriculum and Classroom Activities

Overview of the chapter

Curricula and the meeting of minds

The curriculum and its associated activities together constitute a set of classroom conditions – the main ground for the meeting of minds between teachers and learners. In this chapter, we look at the special features of these conditions that enable teachers and learners to make diverse connections for literacy instruction. In the first part, we examine how curricula can make a meeting of minds relatively easy or difficult. In the second part, we explore the special characteristic of activities that determines how teachers and learners can connect effectively with each other.

A working definition of curriculum

Darling-Hammond describes a curriculum as being:

The arrangements a school makes for students' learning and development, including the sequence, format, and content of the courses; student activities; teaching approaches; and the ways in which teachers and classes are organized. (Darling-Hammond, 1997, page 229)

This definition emphasises what *is* done rather than what *is said should be* done. The distinction has been well appreciated in literacy research. Its history is littered with failed attempts to find differences between reading programmes, because what is specified in a curriculum may not indeed be what is taught and is only one part of how teaching and learning are organised.[1]

The description is useful for considering the range of things that make up curricula as they are enacted. It provides a framework that is applicable to any school. However, our purpose is to evaluate how curricula might limit or support the meeting of minds.

Curricula as channels for teaching and learning

What is it about the enacted curriculum that provides arrangements for effective teaching and learning? The analogy that we use here is one of channels. Curricula provide channels of varying width in which teaching and learning occur. They offer routes for development of various kinds. They indicate the goals that are valued and what should be done to reach these goals in the course of development.

Channels in child rearing

A parallel can be drawn with child rearing. We seldom refer to explicit curricula for this, but families nonetheless hold views about the forms of learning and development that they expect and value (Goodnow and Collins, 1990). They will value certain features of development, such as children talking in particular ways. They will have in mind goals for how and when these developments should occur, perhaps becoming concerned if children do not show them at the "right" or "expected" time and being pleased if they show them early.

Jaan Valsiner (1987) uses the concept of a Zone of Promoted Actions to describe how parents promote the things they value – how they construct channels that increase the probability of some actions and decrease the probability of others. This way of doing things – how families arrange, select, and deploy activities consistent with the values they tacitly or explicitly hold – is a specific component of the socialisation model, the framework for describing how literacy happens that we are using in this book.

Channels of varying width

In a similar way, school curricula can be seen as channels for promoting certain sorts of activities and expertise. As such, they can provide channels of varying width. We are going to pay particular attention to that dimension in using this analogy of channels (see Figure 2). Thinking of curricula as channels, the dimension of width is easy to spot if we ask how closely the enacted curriculum specifies what is to be learned.

Figure 2
Curriculum channels
(a) wide channel with concurrent learning

Child learning   *wide channel*

(b) narrow channel with sequential learning

Child learning   *narrow channel*

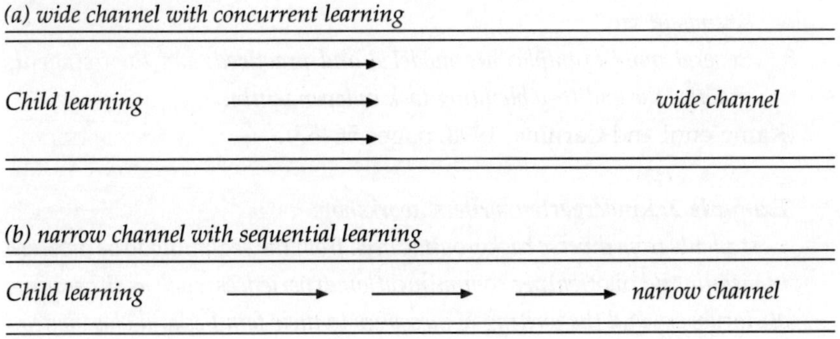

We can perhaps appreciate how width applies when we ask questions of the curriculum as we have defined it. For example, how do arrangements made for the sequences, formats, and content of literacy learning channel children's development? How do specific teaching approaches channel children's development? To what degree do the activities that have been selected, including the forms of assessment, specify in detail a particular sequence of steps to be taken? To what degree does organisation enable a number of developmental sequences and a range of ways of acting to occur concurrently and simultaneously?

Wide and narrow curricula

To apply the idea of width to the curricula of literacy instruction, we can illustrate the extremes in this dimension with two examples. In the first, the authors are describing one part of a highly specific curriculum. In the second, the author is outlining principles for a comparatively non-specific curriculum.

Example 1: *Steps specified in an instructional strategy for auditory blending at the phonemic awareness stage:*

Focusing (in beginning instruction) on phonemic awareness, alphabetic understanding, and automaticity with the code will allow instructional designers to focus on what is instructionally important and empirically validated ... to achieve more efficient and effective outcomes for beginning readers with diverse learning needs ....

1   *The teacher models sounds in words: "Listen carefully as I say the sounds in run. I will say each sound, but I will not stop between sounds: /rrrrruuuuunnnnn/; run."*

2   *The children practice the sounds: "Let's try one together. Let's say the sounds in sat."*

3   *Several more examples are modeled and practiced, and then students practice the auditory blending task independently.*

(Kame'enui and Carnine, 1998, pages 56–57).

Example 2: *Kindergarten writers' workshop:*

... students from diverse backgrounds need from the beginning to be involved in meaningful, motivating communication experiences, such as the reading of storybooks and the writing of messages to their families and classmates

.... Ronald ... always did drawings showing events involving his family and friends. Although some of the other students used invented spelling along with their drawings, Ronald relied on drawings alone to communicate his message. As the year went on, with the assistance of the teacher and other students, Ronald began to use invented spelling to label his drawings. At first, he wrote just a letter for the initial sound in a word, such as B for brother. *By the end of the year he was able to compose sentences using invented spelling.* (Au, 1993, pages 38–41).

In the first example of a contemporary literacy curriculum, the authors specify a sequence of stages for reading instruction through which children should progress, the argument being that mastery of one stage is a prerequisite for the next. In this kind of highly specified curriculum, the instructional steps in each stage are prescribed, as are the steps in component tasks. By contrast, the curriculum described in the second example promotes the teaching and learning of a variety of components concurrently and within a less clearly specified and sequenced set of tasks.

Limitations of narrow curricula

The first of the two examples above represents a very narrow curriculum and the second a very wide one. There are strengths and weaknesses associated with both of these extremes, which we will explore later. However, there are two problems associated with narrowly specified curricula that impinge on the business of making connections – on how we incorporate children's diversity in teaching and learning.

If we think of curricula as channels of varying width, it follows that the wider the channel, the greater the diversity of skills and knowledge that it can accommodate. Therefore, the problems associated with a narrow curriculum come in two forms: its limitations on teachers and its limitations on learners.

Limitations on teachers

Narrow curricula reduce teachers' capability to teach for diversity, to connect. From her review of effective teaching, Darling-Hammond (1998) argues that flexibility, adaptability, and creativity are among the most important determinants of teachers' effectiveness. Her argument is supported by researchers of change processes in schools (Fullan, 2001).

In Darling-Hammond's own studies, teachers have consistently rejected highly prescribed curricula as undermining their own sense of professionalism and their ability to teach effectively. However, not all teachers feel like this. A number of teachers in her reports appreciated having a high degree of guidance. Theirs is a very important concern – it reflects the potential problems in a wide curriculum.

Limitations on learners

Narrow curricula can have unwanted effects on children, too. One is that a narrowly defined set of tasks reduces children's ability to transfer their learning. Generally speaking, the more closely specified and constrained (for example, in component steps) the task is, the harder it is for learners to apply their learning to similar tasks. Demonstrations of this phenomenon are as old as the history of experimental psychology and come from both the laboratory and the classroom.[2]

When students are presented with tasks as isolated bits to be learned, they have little understanding of the overall goals or outcomes when the bits are added together. They may be able to repeat and demonstrate what they have learned in contexts closely resembling those in which they learned them, but they often cannot use this information in novel circumstances or to connect ideas across lessons, subjects, or domains of thought.

A curriculum that promotes only segmented, isolated, and elemental learning tasks reduces the student's degree of learning (including incidental learning) and also their preparedness for future learning.[3]

Another problem lies in what a narrow curriculum reduces access to, particularly for culturally and linguistically diverse children.[4] In literacy, in Luis Moll's view (1999), such a curriculum further reduces the opportunities to learn the very things that such students need, including cognitively complex skills and a rapidly expanding vocabulary.

A wide – but not a vague – curriculum

The argument here is that building on the familiar depends on a wide curriculum, but not one that is unclear or lacks careful design. Similarly, we shall see that the clear specification of classroom tasks for children is critical for overcoming the discontinuities between the uses of literacy at home and school and requires children being taught to understand the rules of classroom activities (Hemphill and Snow, 1996). It is the resolution of this tension – between the freedom to invent, adapt, and modify instruction and the risk of ambiguity and lack of specificity and clarity of outcomes – that is central to this book.

Classroom activities and the meeting of minds

How does a wide curriculum that allows for building on the familiar actually happen in classrooms? Curricula are implemented through particular activities, so the means for achieving the goals of a wide curriculum are the activities in which teachers and learners participate. In this section, we explore the nature of certain types of literacy activities in the early stages of literacy instruction. These are activities with one outstanding property – a high degree of versatility, a property that can act like a powerhouse in making connections for any learner, particularly those in culturally and linguistically diverse classrooms.

The characteristics of versatile activities

Versatile activities can have one general form but potentially several different roles. To illustrate this, we can compare the activity of a teacher reading books to students with that of a teacher using exercises outside books to teach students specific phoneme–grapheme relationships.

For example, a session of reading to children involves using a book as a tool, with someone, usually the teacher, reading aloud from the text and the children participating, usually by listening and engaging in discussion. A session of exercises for phonological knowledge involves using a presentation such as a task sheet as a tool and someone, usually the teacher, making statements and the children participating, usually by responding.

Forms and roles

The overall *form* of an activity can be seen in what a teacher and learner generally do to get the business done. Despite some similarities to do with control and direction, the form of what teachers and learners do in each of the activities described above looks distinctly different.

The *roles* that these activities can play vary considerably, too, and this is where we can highlight the property of versatility. An activity's roles can be seen in what the activity accomplishes for the teacher and the student – the ways in which the teacher and learner engage and use knowledge and the things that can be learned from the activity.

What distinguishes the versatility of the two activities above is what can usually be taught and learned through them. In the first, what can be learned is things to do with books and their reading, and in the second, things to do with sound–letter relationships. One activity has potentially multiple roles and learning outcomes. The other, more constrained, activity has potentially fewer roles and learning outcomes.

Versatility in action

Versatility in an activity comes about because of two elements. One is the interactions – the range of ways in which teachers and students interact during the activity and the ideas that they have about their purposes while they are interacting. These create the roles of the activities. The other is the figuring out – the range of opportunities that the activity provides for children to work out, in their own minds, their ideas about the literacy tool that they are using and to invent ways of engaging in the activity.

These two elements are what make versatility so important for the classroom instruction that aims to provide a fruitful meeting ground for the minds of learners and teachers. We will now look at them in more detail.

Interactions in versatile activities

Literacy activities vary considerably in the range of interactions they allow. Here, for example, are some extracts from story-reading sessions with children in family and early childhood settings involving Māori and Pacific Islands children in New Zealand.

This example comes from one family reading two different books to a child who is almost five years old.

Text 1: Patch had been given the job of painting white lines for the running lanes.
Reader (interrupts reading): What are they doing there, D...?
Child: Painting ... a line.
Reader: So that they can run down the track straight. (Resumes reading.)
Text 2: Andrew had an engine called Red Streak.

Reader: Andrew.
Child: Andrew.
Reader: had.
Child: had.
Reader: an engine.
Child: an engine.
(McNaughton, 1995, page 112)

These examples come from teachers reading books to a group of nearly five-year-old children in a kindergarten.

T: Three little bears. One with a...
C: Light.
T: One with a ...
C: Stick.
T: And one with a ...
C: Rope.
    ...
Text (teacher reading): The bear couldn't believe his ears. He gulped and sniffed and wiped his tears. "You can talk after all," he cried.
T: He has got little ears hasn't he. Yes, he has got little ears, what about Eddy?
C: Big ears.
T: Has he not got little ears, what about you?
C: No, you have got big ears.
T: I have got big ears, yes, I know.
C: I have got little ones.
T: You have got little ears, yes dear.
    ...
Text (teacher reading): Don't be scared, you're my teddy. "No, I'm not," cried the voice. "It's me, Eddy."
T: Look at the look on his face.
C: Aaaa big face.
T: Mmmmm
C: Big face.
T: Yes, he has got a big face.
C: A little face.

T: Little teddy bear.
T: Oh, what about this one here?
C: Big face, a fat face.
T: He looks a bit worried doesn't he?
C: This is a fat face.

   ...

T: What is he doing here?
C: Mmmm holding teddy.
T: He is holding his teddy. What is he doing with his other hand?
C: Scratching his nose.
T: He is scratching his nose.
C: Yeah.
T: I think it looks to me that he has his thumb in his mouth.
(Phillips, McNaughton, and MacDonald, 2001, pages 67–69)

Obviously, from these examples, the activity "reading a storybook" varies greatly in its interactions, in their manner and purpose, across different people, across different books, and even within one book. Sometimes the child fills a gap left by the reader or repeats what the reader says. At other times there are questions and answers about the sizes of objects in an illustration. At yet other times there is discussion about the meaning of what is happening and how the participants feel. There is obviously a relationship between such variability and the versatility of the activity. To understand the nature of this variability more precisely, we need to describe activities in greater detail.

Activities in finer detail
Activities can be defined more precisely than we have thus far by describing their specific features. These include the ways of participating and the forms of guidance that they offer, the goals for carrying them out held by participants, and the range of expertise developing from the activity (McNaughton, 1995). In these examples of reading stories to children, we can detect variations in goals, ways of participating, forms of guidance, and learning outcomes – these all create different roles for the activity.[5] The variations are detectable between different examples of reading and in moment-to-moment shifts during a reading session.

Reading to children – various styles for various purposes

Family members or teachers tend to switch, often with great dexterity, between three main styles in their interactions to serve different purposes in their reading (McNaughton, 1995). The styles can be described respectively as narrative, performance, and item learning.

In the narrative style, the focus of child and reader is primarily on the story, its characters, the events, the action as it unfolds, and the relationships between the text and the participants' own experiences. The interactions are like conversations in which the reader erects a kind of scaffolding to guide the child into understanding what the text means.

The performance style focuses on developing children's ability to recite portions of the text, maintaining the authority of the text through accurate reproduction of the words.

The item learning style is concerned with conveying items of knowledge that arise from the text such as colours, letters, or labels. Skills in identifying the items, as well as specific knowledge of them, are achieved through questioning routines initially controlled by the person reading the book.

Over time, and with familiar books, these styles provide the basis for particular sorts of expertise to develop. The narrative style, for example, is associated with ways of comprehending texts that have similarities with the comprehension strategies valued at school (Dickinson and Tabors, 2001). The performance style is associated with (among other things) recitation memory, and the item learning style, particularly with young children, with learning to label objects and attributes such as colours (McNaughton, 1995).[6]

Opportunities for construction in versatile activities

The other major element in an activity's versatility is the range of opportunities that it provides learners to figure out their ideas about what the activity is offering them and to invent ways of engaging in what is happening – their capacity for construction.

Children construct ideas about their world through their own actions, their interactions with others, and their reflections and inventions from their observations. This goes for all the activities in which they participate. They develop their own ideas about the nature and purposes of what they are engaged in. Some of these ideas can be directly traced to those things that are made explicit. Others have gone beyond what was made explicit as the children make their own sense of what they have experienced and what has occurred.

Going beyond what is given

By its very nature, any activity provides opportunities for what Bruner (1980) calls "going beyond the information given". However, activities are inherently different in the range of opportunities that they provide for this to take place. The range varies from very narrow activities that offer little possibility of going beyond what is given, to very wide activities that provide huge scope for ideas and ways of acting, both appropriate and inappropriate.

The scope of what is given – narrow and wide examples

For example, the range of incidental things that may be learned when a teacher uses the Elkonin technique in Reading Recovery is relatively small.[7] Clay and Cazden (1990) provide an example of a teacher using this procedure during the activity of composing a story. Six-year-old Pramela wants to, but can't, write "hen made" in the sentence, "The little red hen made some cakes". With the teacher prompting, Pramela says the words slowly "h-e-n, m-a-d-e". She then has to push counters into boxes that the teacher draws corresponding to the number of sounds (phonemes) that can be heard in the words.

The following example comes from an interaction with a Māori child in the first days of school. The child has a much-loved cat called Samantha, which she wants to write about. The teacher has set up a session in which children write about topics, and she circulates around the class carrying out individual conferences:

Teacher: What is that letter?
Child: [S]
Teacher: And that letter?
Child: [m]
Teacher: Good girl. What are you going to write?
Child: Samantha.
Teacher: Samantha. Oh, your little cat. Is that what you are trying to write – Samantha?
Child: Yea.

Teacher: Good girl. Tell me about Samantha. Write your story. I'll leave you to it.
(later)
Teacher: How about writing something about Samantha? You start 'Samantha'. What are you going to write about Samantha?
Child: Samantha is sick.
Teacher: Samantha is sick. Would you like to write that?
(Goodridge, 1995, page 304)

The first example comes from a Reading Recovery session designed as a one-on-one intervention with children making low rates of progress. The session involves text reading and writing and other activities as well as this specific teaching of letter–sound relationships. Here is a situation where close specification may be very appropriate to guarantee the needed learning in the context of a wider curriculum.

The second example shows a session that provides some opportunities for the child to pick up ideas about terms such as "letter", "writing", and "story", some of which may be appropriate to general conventional school knowledge and some of which may not (for example, the idea of what counts as a "story").

The scope in activities for incidental learning

The two examples are not meant to suggest that one is right and the other is wrong. Rather, they illustrate how activities with narrow and wide specifications relate to incidental learning. In circumstances where a learner has experienced difficulties with learning some concepts, close specification for some item learning can be very appropriate, as the success of Reading Recovery demonstrates.

In some activities, such as a writing conference, the role of the learner in picking up new knowledge can be substantial and substantially different from what the teacher might expect. Incidental learning can be extensive under appropriate conditions. Children can also acquire substantial knowledge and awareness of phoneme–grapheme relationships during writing conferences, even though the curriculum elsewhere may not provide much explicit teaching of this knowledge beyond reading books and writing texts.[8]

Picking up vocabulary

A powerful demonstration of what students can be incidentally learning, comes from research into vocabulary learning during reading texts. The phenomenon is so pervasive that predictable relationships can be described. One meta-analysis examined incidental learning of new word meanings where there are no instructions to read for this purpose (Swanborn and de Glopper, 1999). It was found that, under ordinary personal reading conditions, students reading typical books will spontaneously work out and learn the meaning of about fifteen in every one hundred unknown words they encounter. Even readers at the beginning of instruction can do this (McNaughton, 1987). The higher the grade level, the more students can pick up, and students with high reading ability (including larger vocabularies) learn more word meanings.

Managing the uses of activities – dangers and dilemmas

Activities vary considerably in the versatility of their roles. However, the advantage of highly versatile activities is that they can be made focused and constrained. The reverse does not apply – activities of limited versatility can not be other than limited. That is what they are.

However, this quality of versatility also poses dangers for effective instruction, creating a set of dilemmas for teachers to solve. Highly versatile activities have great potential for making connections between teachers and culturally and linguistically diverse learners. They also have great potential for discriminating against diversity by making tasks difficult to fathom (Delpit, 1995). Closely specified activities potentially enable learners and teachers to focus on what needs to be learned, but that quality also increases the risk of limitations to the learning. These tensions are significant in the process of meeting of minds. They produce three specific dilemmas.

Dilemma 1: Managing prior knowledge

The first dilemma is that highly versatile activities are user-friendly for those who already know things about the activity and potentially discriminatory against those who do not. This is where the Matthew effects can be seen at work. The more a student knows – about conventional school literacy, about the topic in a text, or about the ways of talking and uses of language in classrooms – the more incidental learning can take place. This relationship is a basic principle in learning – what you already know primes you for what you can learn from an activity.

The relationship is illustrated in the studies of incidental learning while reading. All other things being equal (such as difficulty levels of texts), of every one hundred unknown words that they encounter, low ability readers will gain about 0.75 words, average ability readers will gain about twelve, and high ability readers will gain about nineteen.

This dilemma can be resolved by the teacher managing activities to maximise the knowledge and skills that a child brings to them and increasing a child's understanding of what activities require. Strategies for managing activities are discussed in Chapter 3, and strategies for increasing understanding are introduced in Chapter 7.

Dilemma 2: Knowing the goals for each participant

The second dilemma is that the effective use of activities with high versatility requires more expertise from teachers than the effective use of activities with limited versatility. The more open and versatile the activity, the greater its potential for confusion, ambiguity, and lack of common understanding of its goals by teacher and learners. Teachers need to be keenly aware of the instructional focus of the activity and "where the child is at". The resolution of this dilemma is addressed in Chapters 5 and 9, where we discuss the nature of teachers' expertise.

Dilemma 3: Getting the balance right

The third dilemma comes from the need for teachers to be flexible and strategic in their use of activities that vary in versatility. Children need to learn letter–sound relationships, alphabetical and other kinds of item knowledge, and comprehension strategies. Teachers need to judge when to switch activities and when to adapt them so as to guarantee that learning takes place as effectively as possible for further progress.

But in putting constraints on highly versatile activities or by using very specific ones, the teacher needs to adjust the balance so that skills can be transferred and incidental learning can take place. The resolution of this dilemma is discussed in detail in our treatment of the teaching of phonics (Chapter 4) and the teaching of comprehension (Chapter 8).

End Notes

1   See Pressley, Rankin, and Yokoi (1996) and Darling-Hammond (1997).

2   The studies of Thorndike and his colleagues in 1901 could be used as the benchmark for this – see Bransford and Schwartz (1999).

3   See Brown (1994), Gardner (1991), and Bransford and Schwartz (1999). In the literacy field, Bussis (1982) describes incongruous results produced by highly scripted, test-based early reading curricula. He reports children who have the measurable skills but still fail to read, and proficient readers who sometimes cannot demonstrate mastery of the "prerequisite" reading skills.

4   See Bartolome (1998), Darling-Hammond (1997), and Delpit (1995).

5   Previously, I have described these variations as creating distinct activities. It seems more helpful to see the overall form as one activity and its variations as creating distinctly different roles for the general form.

6   In several studies in New Zealand, these styles have been observed used by various families, including indigenous Māori, and Pākehā (of Anglo-European descent) families, and first- and second-generation Pacific Islands families. The studies show that when storybooks are the vehicle and children are three and four years old, Pākehā families tend to use the narrative style. With other families, particularly Pacific Islands families, the performance style is often used. Qualifications need to be placed on these sorts of summaries. The variation within a cultural group in their uses of different styles can be greater than the variation between groups (McNaughton, 1996). But the studies indicate a tendency for Pākehā families to be more exclusive in their use of the narrative style and for Māori and Pacific Islands families to be more dexterous in using the different styles.

7   With this technique, the teacher teaches a child to listen for and represent the number of sounds that they hear by placing counters representing the sounds into boxes. See Clay (1993).

8   See McIntyre and Freppon (1994) and Tunmer and Chapman (1997).

Chapter 3

Strategies for Incorporating the Familiar

Overview of the chapter

The business of incorporation

In this chapter, we explore the strategies that teachers use in effective literacy instruction to build on what is familiar for culturally and linguistically diverse children. A strategy in this sense is an instructional approach, adaptable to circumstances and flexibly employed, that a teacher will use to meet teaching goals. The strategies discussed here all have the same goal – to connect literacy instruction in the classroom with the experience and expertise that a child brings to school from family and community activities.

Getting the measure of children's expertise

At the beginning of their formal literacy instruction, children have varying levels of expertise in literacy, and this expertise comes in a variety of forms. Teachers can find out where children are at with some of these forms when they give the standard tests of conventional school literacy to them. Such forms include recognition of the letters of the alphabet or whole words, knowledge of letter–sound relationships, and concepts about print.

But these forms of expertise represent a thin slice of a child's skills and knowledge on entry to school. Other forms have developed in family and community activities. Teachers need to identify forms of all kinds and ensure a place for them in the classroom. Their ways for going about this are what we call here strategies of incorporation.

Segregating home from school

Fran Perkins graphically describes her own experience of a situation where the forms of home language and literacy are segregated from those of school:

> *Unlike the language learning experiences in my school, my home was filled with extremely valuable literacy experiences that were crucial to the culture of my home and community. My siblings and I were afforded the opportunities to memorize and deliver speeches (or recitations) for Church and community programs. My parents' major contributions to our literacy development existed in the form of telling stories about their childhoods and encouraging us to entertain each other with our own. Subsequently, this led to my siblings and me telling our own stories (exaggerated versions of our parents', initially) for enjoyment. There was nothing as entertaining as my older sisters' renditions of poems .... Unfortunately, very few of these literacy events were valued in the language arts*

programs that were prominent in my elementary school years. Although these experiences were valuable to me and a crucial part of my culture, they were never viewed as real reading by the school, my family, or me. Therefore, when given an occasional choice to read in school, I didn't. I always perceived the act of reading in school as reading someone else's story with pictures that were only vaguely connected to the words. (Perkins, 1999, page 48)

Enabling home uses of language and literacy to permeate classroom instruction and to be built on is the business of incorporation. One of the premises of this book is that teaching and learning can be made more effective if teachers can incorporate the range of expertise brought to the school by culturally and linguistically diverse children. Without the classroom conditions that we described in Chapter 2, it is difficult to employ the appropriate strategies. But without deliberately employing the strategies, those conditions are weak devices for ensuring effective teaching.

The strategies that we describe come in four main forms: using classroom texts for reading and writing; using familiar activities; using familiar forms of discourse; and incorporating cultural values and meanings into pedagogy. The forms overlap and have common elements. But separating them out enables us to see more clearly what makes them effective and what evidence there is for this.

Strategies using classroom texts for reading and writing

Teachers can use texts for reading, and writing, as avenues for incorporation. Activities that involve reading and writing texts are sufficiently versatile for teachers to be able to plan and implement instruction through them in ways that increase the likelihood of a meeting of minds. The strategies can work with features such as content, language, and illustration in text, both separately and together.

With each of these features, it is possible to incorporate the experiences and expertise personal to a child. It is also possible to incorporate knowledge and skills that are more common to a child's community and cultural group or the wider society in which they live. However, the primary focus for building on the familiar is a particular child's experiences and uses of language and literacy.

Familiar content

One of the most familiar and frequently reported strategies of incorporation uses the content of texts, in both writing and reading activities, to capture recognisable parts of a student's experiences.

New Zealand's Native Schools

Examples of the strategy abound in the history of the Native Schools for Māori in New Zealand. Established in rural Māori communities by the state education department in the late nineteenth century, the schools had early policy and practices that included Māori language as a medium of instruction, though this was soon replaced by English. However, many teachers rejected the imported texts provided by the education authorities for reading instruction as inadequate for children whose first language was Māori. These teachers often wrote their own, using local topics and settings. The accounts of two Pākehā (Anglo-European) teachers from the 1920s and the 1940s provide examples:

> *When I went to this [Native School] I was shocked. I looked at the reading material and it was the old Blackie's phonic readers .... The material was so foreign from anything Māori ... I wrote to the Department and said ... I couldn't possibly use them for reading. ... They wrote back and said, well, if the Department has piles of these books on the shelves you just have to keep on using them. So I burnt the lot and I just had to make my own materials.* (Teacher starting in her first Native School, 1928)
>
> *I particularly concentrated on reading because in those days reading was an empty dreary dull subject – the old Beacon readers were the texts and they were 50 years old. Māori kids learning about English squirrels and nightingales – just meaningless. So I wrote my own text and in those days you'd introduce one word per page and then all the other words had to be words that had already been introduced. You kept the words to a minimum .... I used the local scene and it was a very good series of readers ... the stories were very good.* (Teacher in a Native School, 1944)
> (McNaughton, 2001, page 108)

Teachers reported local texts of this kind to be effective. Some general survey data from the 1930s also suggests that the teaching of comprehension in English in the Native Schools was more effective than teaching in the mainstream state schools. The experiences with these sorts of text contributed to the development of "natural language" texts published by the Department of Education in two generations of the core reading series Ready to Read.[1]

African American third-graders

Perkins (1999) reported on teachers' deliberate selection and use of commercially available books written, from an insider's perspective, for African American students. Her transcripts from grade three classrooms in a low-income urban community record children making extended responses to books that have family themes and intergenerational relationships. The quality and engagement of these responses point to the part played by the children's familiarity with the topics and experiences.

Example, reading *Aunt Flossie's Hats and Crab Cakes Later.*

T.P.: It made me feel good inside.

Teacher: Tell us more.

T.P.: It made me feel good how she [Aunt Flossie] told the stories and how the story was about way back then. My mama tells me stories from way back then, and my grandmama.

Teacher: What kinds of stories do they tell?

T.P.: She [my grandmother] said one time that she never had no daddy because her daddy ... died before she came into the world. And she told me about that.

   ...

K.L.: My grandmama has lots of hats.

S.T.: My grandmama wear [s] hats to church and stuff.

Teacher: I remember my mama wearing hats in church, too.

T.P.: My mama [has] hats everywhere – in the closet, in my room. But we can't wear [them].

(Perkins, 1999, page 54)

The evidence here is of engagement, enjoyment, discussion, and commentary – interactions of a kind, Perkins argues, not often associated with teaching these students. But how do such connections contribute to literacy learning? How do teachers build on this familiarity to enable children to comprehend and produce texts in school-related ways?

As Perkins's example shows, it happens when events and topics familiar to a child are built into texts and when teachers are aware of how to create space for children's voices to be heard and can manage dialogue so that children's language resources are "resituated" or "recontextualised" in school-like forms (Dyson, 1999a).

Grade two writers

Dyson shows the role of the teacher in this process when she describes, in her accounts of writing in a grade two classroom, how a "permeable" curriculum creates space for children to produce, present, explain, and edit their texts. Writing time occurred in the classroom daily. It comprised a composing period, followed by free writing and then by either "author's theatre", in which the writers could choose classmates to act out their stories, or "author's chair", where they could read their stories.

The classroom had a mixture of children from economically poor, predominantly African American communities and more affluent European American communities. During "author's theatre", the teacher (Kristin) spotlighted texts and authorial decisions in pursuit of her goal to encourage and improve writing. In the following example, Kevin has written a story of teenage mutant ninja turtles and X-men. He presents a picture to the class and reads the conversational blurbs:

Kevin: "WOW!" "AHHHHH" "OUCH!"

Kristin: Do you have some narrative that goes along with it and tells [the actors] what to do? Can you make some up?

Kevin: Well, I didn't have time to finish it so it says "to be continued".

(Kevin exploits the text's function as memory support: unlike [another child], *he does not stray from what is written.)*

(After the performance is over, Seth and then Radha comment on their lack of anything to do.)

Kristin: Remember what happened the other day, when somebody said, "These are the people in my class", and they just stood there. What did we say about that?

LaShanda: [No] action.

Kristin: We asked about adding action. We said that if you had an essay ... if you had something that didn't have action in it, you should share it in Author's Chair. In Author's Theater, we have all the action. Well, Kevin had action in his. But what happened? Jonathan?

Jonathan: I think it was a really good play because I liked my part. And – like – it was sort of like telling about the thing, and then you could – like – tell

about all of 'em, and then you could get moving and do the story.
Kristin: OK, so you're saying it was a good beginning for the play, right?
(Dyson, 1995, page 39)

Dyson describes how, throughout this episode, the teacher maintained her focus on teaching the children to write, introducing conceptual tools and the vocabulary used by authors and needed by the audience ("narrative", "action", "essay"). In another example, the teacher uses queries such as, "Was your writing any different this time from what it was the last time, or was it the same?" Following discussion, she asks, "So, will you write that into [your text] for next time?"

Identification of interests

Further support for the strategy's effectiveness comes from experimental studies of the effects of interest on comprehension. In a review of motivational processes in text comprehension (Guthrie and Wigfield, 1999), the researchers found that when students identify more closely with the topics and experience presented in texts, they become more personally interested in the material. Higher levels of personal interest can produce increased comprehension and learning through more extensive cognitive processing. In another study (Cordova and Leeper, 1996), the researchers incorporated personal details of a task into the text by using nicknames, names of friends, favourite foods, hobbies, television shows, books, and magazines. This "personalisation" of the task had effects on children's learning, their task involvement, their motivation to engage in the reading task, and their level of aspiration to read effectively.

Familiar language

Familiarity of language is obviously closely related to familiarity of content, and separating the use of familiar language from that of content in texts can be somewhat artificial. However, the language of the children who are central to this book may often be a variety of English that is systematically different from the standard English forms used in books and valued in the classroom. Different does not necessarily mean less complex or less effective language. But the curriculum as it is enacted can implicitly, even explicitly, discriminate against children's non-standard language and therefore their identity (Au, 1993).

The use of familiar words is a straightforward form of incorporation. It is not only possible to incorporate familiar content into the standard language of texts, it is also possible to incorporate children's own forms of language. For example, writing local texts in New Zealand's Native Schools also meant using local vocabulary, local sentence structures, and local idioms.

> *Because the language was so artificial … it didn't have any meaning. It didn't have [the] emotion involved and I was dealing with people who were all emotion and I wanted to actually write books that were written the way the children spoke. And I did …. When the children wrote their stories, that's what I wrote.* (McNaughton, 2001, page 109)

There are many instances in Dyson's studies (1999b, for example) of this strategy at work in student writing, with the children reinventing and playing with language forms as they write. Other studies (Bull, 1996, for example) have shown how children's everyday language, such as Black English, can be incorporated into a writing programme effectively. The issue faced by teachers here is, again, to enable children over time to become fluent in the standard English forms used in classrooms. Au (1993) argues that this fluency should properly be a goal of, not a precursor to, effective instruction. Developing this kind of dual fluency can confer advantages to children whose subsequent proficiency in multiple forms provides a basis for increased awareness and control of the various forms.

Evidence from systematic research shows that using children's own words, at least those that are rich in meaning and imagery for them, assists the children to learn sight words in reading texts (Hiebert and Martin, 2001). But there is little research on the use of different dialect forms in beginning reading texts as a basis for more effective literacy instruction, and what there is has produced mixed results (Snow, Burns, and Griffin, 1998). It may be, as we shall argue in the chapters on awareness strategies, that the incorporation of different dialects at this level may be insufficient and, in some circumstances, confusing. What is needed in addition, or perhaps instead (to reiterate the point made previously) is for teachers to understand and value differences and to teach in ways that enable children to become aware of and control and exploit these differences during instruction.

Familiar illustrations

Illustrations are an integral part of texts for beginning reading. Similarly, many early classroom approaches to children's writing also use children's drawings and pictures. There has been some controversy over how illustrations function as aids to acquiring literacy generally. Research has drawn at least two conclusions. Illustrations do not aid word learning when children are presented with lists of words or sentences. When they accompany texts, however, illustrations can enhance, for example, children's accuracy in reading, their self-regulation (as indicated by their self-corrections), and their comprehension. (McNaughton, 1987).

Research generally supports the usefulness of illustrations in texts for priming children's knowledge of topics and the vocabulary that they can use in reading.[2] But what kind of role can illustrations play in incorporating familiarity for the children with whom we are concerned?

Illustrations as prompts

Carol Lee (2001) describes several forms of "cultural modelling" in the classroom, in which illustrations, among other media, are used as prompts for African American children's language, which can then be crafted into written language. One form involves the use of historical and contemporary pictures of African American scenes. The scenes invoke the children's general knowledge of cultural images and events as well as their personal knowledge of events.

The teacher mediates the children's reactions through large group discussion, recording on the board the vocabulary and phrases that arise. The children, in pairs, then continue to write. Conferences with the teacher enable them to draw on and develop their use of writing conventions such as punctuation and sentence formation. Under these conditions, the use of cultural modelling improves the quality of writing.[3]

Illustrations and identity

Familiarity in images is like familiarity in content and language. It can range from the highly personal to the kind of background that comes from being a member of a multicultural society. Illustrations can feature prominently in the ways that children make sense of their cultural and personal identities. For example, how Māori children see (or, as

McLachlan (1996) observed, do not see) Māori being portrayed in illustrations is important in the development of positive self and group identity. Moreover, representations of Māori contribute to the views children in general develop about being Māori.

The engaging familiarity of texts

Research on the "engagingness" of texts – their potential to involve the reader – supports how familiarity works together with and enhances the combined effects of content, language, and illustrations in texts. In one study (Hoffman, McCarthy, Abbott, Christian, Corman, Curry, Dressman, Elliot, Matherne, and Stahle, 1994), kindergarten children rated a selection of textbooks. They identified the same features as the researchers for potential to engage them, notably the design (illustrations and format), content, and language. In addition, the children underlined the significance of familiarity (with the author, text, and vocabulary in the text), personal experience with the content, and the realism of the text.

Strategies using familiar activities

What if children arrive at school with little experience of reading for meaning or of writing texts for the usual purposes of classrooms? For some children, these activities are not familiar, and literacy expertise has been forming in other kinds of activities. This is essentially the concern expressed in Perkins' account of her school experience. In her perception, memorising and delivering recitations and making up and telling family stories were not part of classroom literacy.

This situation has been documented by researchers in different communities in various countries. In New Zealand, for example, we can describe ways of using books and writing by Pacific Islands families that do not figure prominently in classrooms. Can children's expertise in family and community activities, such as reciting texts, travel into classrooms?

Rap song analysis

Lisa Delpit reports a teacher deliberately employing as a basis for instruction not just the topics, experiences, and language components with which children are familiar, but also the familiar activities themselves. In her example, an exceptional educator (of older children in this case) incorporated activities from outside the classroom into literacy instruction.

> ... *when she was working with black high school students classified as "slow learners", [she] had the students analyze rap songs to discover their underlying patterns. The students became the experts in explaining to the teacher the rules for creating a new rap song. The teacher then used the patterns the students identified as a base to begin an explanation of the structure of grammar, and then of Shakespeare's plays. Both student and teacher are expert at what they know best.* (Delpit, 1995, page 33)

The teacher here was mediating the activity in order to enable a higher level of awareness to develop in her students. (See Chapter 7 for further discussion of this instructional approach.)

Family homework

An example of cleverly incorporating elements of a family activity into classroom activities comes from Moll (1999), again with older children. There were two parts to the strategy. One was to identify a frequently occurring literacy activity in the children's homes (in which Spanish was the first language). In the case of these students, it was their homework itself. The second was to design a classroom writing activity that could incorporate the home literacy activity.

The activity selected was to do some expository writing about bilingualism. The students developed a questionnaire, and the assignment for homework was to tap the ideas that family and community members had about bilingualism. The students' essays subsequently incorporated knowledge collected from their community. Homework assignments in which families were involved were therefore the source of content that could be incorporated back into the classroom. The result could be seen as having a kind of double-whammy effect in which both topic and activity found a place at home and at school.

The teacher in Moll's study organised lessons for the assignment so that the students' difficulties with English were minimised while the use of their knowledge of the topic and other experiences was maximised. The teacher provided structured help through drafting and revision to complete goals, enabling curriculum skills such as gleaning data, information, opinions, and simple statistics to develop.

Bringing school books home

Moll's double-whammy strategy has a parallel for young children in the practice of teachers sending early reading books home for children to read to family members. In many families of linguistically and culturally diverse children, this involves the family having to incorporate an unfamiliar activity within a familiar setting (increasing the connections at home – a complementary approach to the meeting of minds). The children's reading thus recreates as a home activity an activity that already exists in classrooms in the form of instructional oral reading. The home-based activity then becomes a part of that activity at school.

There is considerable evidence that this activity, under appropriate conditions, increases the levels of accuracy and self-regulation in oral reading at school. The conditions are that:

- books sent home have already been introduced to the reader and can be read with a high degree of accuracy;
- family members share beliefs and actions with the teacher about the purposes and ways of hearing reading;
- there is two-way communication between family members and teachers about the activity (McNaughton, 1995).

The bonus of this kind of strategy, of course, and one that this book can only touch on, is that when educators work with family members to complement school-like tasks in their home activities, this in itself can produce a kind of reverse incorporation.

Home activities and classroom relevance

The strategy of incorporating home activities depends on using highly versatile classroom activities as the vehicle while keeping a firm eye on the home activities' relevance to classroom goals. In Moll's homework project, for example, he used writing for communication, a highly versatile activity, to incorporate the familiar, but he still maintained the focus on purposeful activities that were relevant to school.

Moll points out, however, that a narrow focus on relevance can lead teachers to use what he calls "reductionist" teaching practices for students with low levels of proficiency in English. These concentrate on the students learning items and simple skills (on the ground that they are what the students need); for example, through completing task sheets rather than writing for a real purpose. This narrowing of the curriculum contributes to a progressive reduction in opportunities for the students to develop higher-level skills – the very ones that they need.

Having said that, though, teachers still need to build in the learning of conventional item knowledge for classroom purposes. This can be done in text activities as well as in discrete item learning activities, as we shall show in the next chapter. But the strategy of incorporating family or community activities may provide a platform for that, too.

Strategies using familiar forms of discourse

We use language for different purposes, and these uses – our discourse – reflect, and help to build, our identities (Schieffelin and Ochs, 1986). Children learn various ways of using language as they are socialised, developing expertise as they become communicating members of their families and communities. Features of this expertise include participation patterns (including when, how, and with whom one talks), communication styles (including timing, rhythm, directness, and use of metaphor), and the variations of dialects. Children's familiarity with their own everyday uses of language can also be incorporated into the discourse of classrooms.

"Talk story" comprehension

The best known, and best researched, example of incorporating home discourse features within early classroom literacy instruction comes from the Kamehameha Early Education Program.[4] Teachers of indigenous Hawaiian children taught them reading comprehension in peer-oriented collaborative groups incorporating "talk story" patterns of interaction. These overlapping, turn-taking patterns of talk are part of the familiar discourse of indigenous Hawaiian children and adults. Results from this approach to teaching comprehension were compared with more typical classroom discourse patterns in which the teacher led and controlled patterns of questions and answers. They showed that the incorporation of "talk story" improved these children's academic engagement and participation.

"Balance of rights" and the Experience–Text-Relationship procedure

This demonstration of improved engagement and participation is significant because it indicates the development among teachers and learners of shared goals and co-ordinated patterns of teaching and learning. The original experimental study and its subsequent replications were part of wider curriculum innovations to do with improving reading scores. One part of this was a classroom organisational principle termed "balance of rights" (Au, 1993). Under this principle, teachers controlled the overall direction of the lesson and its topic and the children controlled the discourse patterns.

Other parts included a sequence of teaching called "Experience–Text-Relationship". In this, the teachers prepare a reading lesson by analysing a story and then selecting a theme for it. The theme chosen will help the children to understand the story as a whole and to problem-solve how the story can be connected to their own background experiences. In the lesson, the story is divided into segments for silent reading and for discussion of the ideas contained in the text. In the relationships phase, the teacher guides the children in making links between their background experience and the ideas in the text.[5] As we shall see in Chapter 9, to work well, it depends on considerable expertise on the part of the teacher.

Personalising oral language

The personalisation possible in beginning reading texts is even more possible in the oral language teachers might use with students. The research previously mentioned on the use of children's names and other familiar words in texts is paralleled by findings on some effective teachers of African American students (Delpit, 1995; Foster, 1995), and teachers in schools with Hispanic children (Cazden, 1988). The former teachers' uses of kin terms and the latter teachers' references to children's well-being and family express a particular kind of alliance and close relationship with students. There are a variety of ways in which teachers might express a respectful relationship with children, but the use of particular community-related terms is one way used by some effective teachers.

Community styles of communication

Delpit also describes how teachers in some African American classrooms use explicit commands in their styles of giving directions rather than the rhetorical and indirect style often used in classrooms. She argues that direct commands match more closely the familiar patterns of adult–child talk in black communities, especially when the adult is an authority figure such as a teacher. The teacher's use of a known style of community discourse establishes that he or she is authoritative through actions rather than through an ascribed role. This in turn helps to establish continuity between home and school.

Another reason why incorporating greater directness like this is useful, Delpit argues, is that the rules for how to do things are made more apparent to the children, an argument to which we shall return in later chapters. Similarly, the effective teachers studied by Gloria Ladson-Billings (see Chapter 4) were fluent in Black English and could switch between Black English and the usual standard English of the classroom and its texts. This "linguistic code-switching" was a skill that teachers taught by both precept and example.

The strategy of using familiar forms of discourse needs to be seen in the context of the whole classroom system built up by teachers and students. For researchers such as Ladson-Billings, the use of community-based communicative styles is one part of developing culturally relevant teaching. Creating particular conceptions of self and others, classroom relations, and knowledge, all help to establish a sense of community within the classroom, a topic we return to in Chapter 8.

Strategies incorporating cultural values and meanings into pedagogy

In some respects, the strategy of pedagogy – the patterns and uses of acts of teaching – is the sum of the previous strategies. The ways in which a teacher teaches carry messages about roles and relationships within the classroom, about what counts as learning, and about what are appropriate uses of language. All of these ways convey messages about one's identity in the classroom, as a learner or a teacher, and how this relates (in degrees of comfort or conflict) to identities outside the classroom.

Directives that work with the culture

Delpit's provocative analysis of effective teaching styles used with African American children highlights the general point. The example she uses in her study is of direct and explicit classroom instructions such as "I don't want to hear it. Sit down, be quiet, and finish your work NOW!" She argues that this displays a high degree of personal power. In her study she contrasts it with the rhetorical and indirect style more typical of European American teachers, for example, "Would you like to sit down now and finish your paper?"

Delpit claims that African American students are likely to obey the explicit directive and ignore the implied directive, because of similarity (in the first instance) with home style and an appropriate display of explicitness and personal power.

Incorporating Kanak cultural practice

Delpit's example brings us to issues of how pedagogies impact on or reflect cultural identities. An analysis of how Kanak culture is incorporated in schools in New Caledonia (Clanche, 1999) highlights the complexity of connecting cultural values to teaching practices. There is a high level of failure for indigenous Kanak students, and in general, both Kanak and European teachers teach these students with the same lack of success.

The schools have made limited connections with Kanak community life, offering supplementary activities such as elders telling stories, singing songs, or lessons on cultural events, for example, the yam cycle. But Pierre Clanche argues there has been little genuine teaching incorporating *la coutume* – the set of perceptions, rules, values, and gestures of offering and receiving that pervades the everyday life of the local culture. Teachers, both Kanak and non-Kanak, need to trust their own cultural resources and incorporate them into their formal practice, as in the following example.

> *The youngest children in a primary school had to go and stay with their penfriends in a distant island. A few days before their flight, they were preparing the customary presents. The schoolmistress drew a grid on the board with columns: Who for? Why? What? Filling in the "Who for?" and "Why?" questions led to expected answers (the chief, the headmistress, families, the mayor). Such was not the case with the "What?" column. For the people with a clearly defined customary assignment, the children chose presents accordingly (mats, fabric, money). For the others, i.e. the people belonging to the schoolchildren's environment, they managed to choose presents taking both the customary*

significance and the persons themselves into account. For the headmistress, who was a nun, they thought of a rosary and for the mayor a cap. (Clanche, 1999, pages 363–364)

Certainly, this example incorporates content from Kanak everyday life. But it also incorporates an element of cultural practice into the life of the classrooms.

Older helps younger

New Zealand's former Native Schools provide other examples, as do some contemporary New Zealand classrooms. An important feature of the Māori cultural world is whanaungatanga, literally "familiness". Many aspects of life, both formal and informal, can be seen as expressions of the need to establish and maintain the functions of extended family. One expression of this has been described as the tuakana–teina relationship, that of an older sibling (or mentor) supporting and assisting a younger sibling (or novice). The significance of these relationships was recognised by the Native School teachers.

> *We found over the years that the best teachers ever in Māori Schools were Māori children. You got the [older] children to help teach the younger ones.* (Teacher in Native Schools, 1947–63)

> *You'd have an older child bringing the younger child into the classroom and the older child might stay with the younger one all day if necessary, until the younger child was happy for the older one to go away. And then some older child in the class would take over.* (Teacher in Native Schools, 1939–59) (McNaughton, 2001, page 98)

Customising classroom practice

In each of the examples given so far, teachers have incorporated particular cultural practices into their pedagogy. This continues to be true of research that has grown out of the earlier Kamehameha Early Education Program studies. Katherine Au, Margaret Maaka, and their colleagues have been developing literacy instruction that incorporates cultural values and processes found in indigenous Hawaiian community settings (Au and Maaka, 1998). Among other activities, readers' and writers' workshops are used as basic vehicles for effective instruction, but they are customised to reflect and build on the cultural identity of the students. Community values are incorporated within these workshops as both topics and ways of interacting; for example, by contributing to the well-being of one's family or friends rather than working only for one's own well-being.

The work of Au and Maaka demonstrates the arguments made in the previous chapter and present in each of the examples. One can connect cultural values to existing curriculum practices if those curriculum practices are versatile enough to incorporate them. It isn't necessary to create new classroom practices.

However, this kind of cultural grafting is effective when the purposes of the classroom activities are not compromised or confused by social practices. This is the reason for the effectiveness of "Talk More" in the Kamehameha Program (Cazden, 1988) and of the use of such principles as whanaungatanga and tuakana–teina in experimental programmes for tutoring in New Zealand.[6]

Making connections – a whole view of strategies

Isolating a set of strategies is useful for the purpose of finding out what works. But it may suggest a mechanical, dispassionate, and piecemeal view of teaching. This is not the intention. The analysis aims to help teachers to become more precise about what they know so that they can be better teachers in the complex and resource-rich world of diverse urban classrooms. The "how" of excellent teaching that makes connections with the children in these classrooms is more than the sum of these strategies. It includes passion and commitment, which, together with strategies, are best seen as a whole.

The sense of wholeness is conveyed powerfully in studies of effective teachers of African American children (see, for example, Foster, 1995; Ladson-Billings, 1994). Each of the specific strategies described in this chapter has been identified in those studies. But, in addition, the teachers studied were described as having "cultural solidarity"; that is, strong attachments to the children and their communities. These teachers exhibited the warmth of acceptance and involvement in personal interactions but had firm control and autonomy, as well as high expectations for effort and achievement. They focused on the whole child, and were concerned for social and emotional well-being and the development of an informed critical awareness of educational, social, and political structures.

This has implications for these teachers' view of content. They were aware that state and local curricula may have failed to include the experiences of African American students and, consequently, may have failed to engage those students in meaningful learning. They purposely designed curricula that made their students (and their heritage) the focus of curriculum inquiry. The content of the curriculum thereby fostered awareness and a critical literacy in the students.

End Notes

1   Sylvia Ashton-Warner (1966) wrote about her experiences and rationales for natural language texts in *Teacher*, the survey data are described in McNaughton (2001), and the development and characteristics of Ready to Read texts are described further in Smith and Elley (1994).

2   How a teacher mediates the use of illustrations in reading clearly makes a difference to their effectiveness. At least one study suggests that the use of illustrations in a shared book activity can confuse rather than inform. If, when they read to children, teachers use illustrations to get the children to predict what a text is about, they may lead the children to think that the task is to guess text from illustrations (Phillips, 1997).

3   Lee argues that there need be no conflict with home oral language in this kind of activity. The point is to develop writing expertise using oral language as expert writers do, crafting from their oral base.

4   See reports and descriptions by Au (1993), Cazden (1988), and Tharp and Gallimore (1988).

5   Many features of the kind of wide curriculum that the Kamehameha Early Education Project represents are associated with effective teaching for all K-3 children, and it is difficult to separate these effects from the effects of incorporation (Snow, Burns, and Griffin, 1998; Goldenberg, 2001). However, while the general curriculum may be effective whatever the cultural context, there is some evidence that incorporation of appropriate features of local discourse should occur to achieve learning outcomes (Cazden, 1988; Goldenberg, 2001).

6   See, for example, the whānau-based Pause, Prompt, and Praise/Tatai, Tautoko, Tautahi programme (Glynn, Berryman, Atvars, and Harawira, 1997).

Chapter 4

Getting a Balance – Incorporation and Phonics

Overview of the chapter

The requirements for balance

Teachers need to be flexible and strategic in their use of activities for making connections with culturally and linguistically diverse children. One of the dilemmas that we noted at the end of Chapter 2 offers teachers a major challenge to their expertise in this. On the one hand, teachers need to teach the specific skills and knowledge that children need to learn. On the other hand, they have to ensure that their classroom activities are as versatile as possible, with ample opportunities for incorporation and incidental learning. They have to keep these requirements in balance. The prime consideration for this balance is to enable learning to take place that gives rise to further learning. Part of this is judging when it is appropriate to switch from one kind of activity to another or to adapt an activity.

In Chapter 3, we looked at how teachers juggle these requirements – their strategies for managing activities that:
- maximise the knowledge and skills that children bring to them;
- keep feeding in the new knowledge and skills that the children need to progress well in their learning.

In this chapter, we focus even more closely on what teachers actually do – the sometimes moment-by-moment switches and adaptations that they make between and within activities, what we call here teaching acts. We look at this in the context of phonics – that set of very specific understandings and skills that all children need to acquire for literacy.

Phonics and the requirements for balance

Phonics is often a hotly debated subject in any discussion of effective early literacy instruction, especially for the children whose needs this book considers. We are not concerned with the polemics of that debate. Rather, we look at how teachers can teach a needed set of specific skills such as phonics and yet continue to enable connections to be made, incorporating what is familiar, in the process.

The balance in literate environments

The balancing of appropriate instructional acts is illustrated in studies by Ladson-Billing (1992; 1994) of effective teachers of African American children. The effective teachers were identified, first by parents and then by principals, against criteria of student achievement, student attitude, parent–teacher interactions, and classroom management. Within her work, there is an analysis of two teachers who were effective teachers of literacy (that is, children in both their classrooms were performing at grade level). One was African American, the other Italian American.

What is compelling about the comparison for our purposes is that the two teachers seemed to use different reading programmes. The first teacher is described as using a "whole language" or literature-based approach to reading. Among other things, children studied texts, discussing plot, characterisation, and words (for example, connotation, denotation), and evaluated text connections (with videos and other books). The second teacher had a more structured approach, using a basal reader series with associated phonics exercises. Her fourth grade lessons appeared to be more scripted and began with phonics drill but had the express purpose of being able to define new words and complex concepts, such as justice, kinsman, and fatigue. This was followed by recapping and retelling stories, making embedded connections with the phonics drill. Like the first teacher, she had round-robin reading, with recall questions again explicitly identifying new and complex vocabulary (for example, atmosphere, influence, and outlet).

Despite the different programme labels, the core of each programme turns out to be very similar, providing a wide curriculum within which different types of teaching occur. Skills were not taught isolated from, or unrelated to, text, and there were many examples of children's real-life experiences being part of the classroom instruction. Ladson-Billings argues that the teachers treated the children as though they already knew things. Their classrooms had other features, to which we return in later chapters:

- the creation of a community of learners with a focus on academic excellence;
- a focus on meaning, comprehension, and critical inquiry;
- high expectations of children's capabilities.

Both teachers work hard to create what might be termed a literate environment. In both classrooms, it is difficult not to become literate. The classrooms are filled with books and various forms of print matter, including trade books, comic books,

pamphlets, journals, magazines, letters and student-developed bulletin boards.
(Ladson-Billings, 1992, page 317)

Environmental phonics

There is a rich description of treating first grade children as if they already know things and building on their knowledge in Shirley Brice Heath's (1983) study of communities and schools. The nineteen African American children in one classroom were already labelled as "potential failures" on reading readiness tests. The teacher developed a programme using the kinds of strategies of incorporation that we have discussed as well as those of enhancing awareness (which we will describe in later chapters).

The strategies for incorporating phonics were imaginative. Many of the families worked in garages around the town. Using old tyres from the garages, the teacher cut out letter shapes and tied them to trees. During the school year, the children were asked to search their neighbourhood for symbols, such as big Ts (telephone poles), upside-down Ls (street light poles). When they rode in their bus to school, they were asked to see which letters they found in objects along the way as well as in ambient print. The classroom focused on recognising the shapes and hearing the sounds of symbols in these familiar contexts.

Clearly, extensive teaching occurred that focused specifically on learning items. But the children's emerging knowledge and awareness of sounds and letters were also incorporated into book-reading activities and writing in the classroom. The phonics teaching was part of a rich programme and, by the end of the school year, all but one child had come up to grade level, and fourteen were above grade level.

Phonics in effective literacy programmes

Larger-scale studies that identify effective literacy instructors echo these smaller case studies. Effective teachers are found to be generally concerned with teaching phonics and use a variety of instructional strategies to teach phonics, irrespective of the programme's label. When detailed observations are made, effective teachers, even in "whole language" classrooms, can be found teaching phonemic and phonological awareness quite explicitly and systematically.[1]

Researchers explored the characteristics of generally effective teachers of literacy in a national sample from the United States (Pressley, Rankin, and Yokoi, 1996). About half of the teachers described themselves as "whole language" teachers, but there were many features common to all of them. These included:

- creating highly literate classroom environments with instruction for lower-order skills and higher-order processes at the earliest levels;
- basic skills often being taught in the context of actual reading and writing with some isolated skills instruction;
- teaching decoding using a variety of procedures, overwhelmingly in the context of real reading.

The authors summarise their descriptions of effective early instruction as a meshing of holistic literacy experiences with skills instruction – the attractive features of a literature- and language-based programme integrated with the acquisition of explicit skills.

This description is reminiscent of some characteristics of classrooms in New Zealand. Research reports over almost two decades suggest that the classroom emphasis is on teaching phonics during guided reading and in writing, in the context of reading and writing texts, with some complementary explicit teaching of phonics in isolation being undertaken as well.[2] Not surprisingly, given the descriptions above, New Zealand has developed a relatively highly effective national programme when seen through the lens of international comparisons, although, for the children who are the focus of this book, it is not effective enough.

Phonics and imbalance

What happens when balanced teaching of the kind that enables children's understanding and expertise to be incorporated into core activities does not occur? Simply adding phonics instruction to a programme does not equal balanced instruction; neither does simply adding opportunities for reading texts and writing. We can illustrate a case of this sort of imbalance by looking at recent literacy instruction in New Zealand schools serving linguistically and culturally diverse children in economically poorer communities.

Trying to patch up the gaps

Over the last thirty years, the instructional programmes in these schools have reflected the general characteristics of good teaching in New Zealand schools. This has included the use of high-interest texts at the core of the reading programme, the extensive use of the activities of reading to children and guided reading instruction, and various forms of process writing and guidance through conferencing as well.

While, overall, children learn to read and write very successfully, and at high levels in international terms, the achievement gaps between Māori and Pacific Islands children in the poorer communities and other children have continued, as we described in Chapter 1. In the face of continuing lower achievement profiles for these children, the schools serving their communities have often added components to their core programmes to boost achievement. This has meant investing in resources for sometimes five or more extras, such as add-on programmes for phonics instruction or for increased community involvement, such as home tutoring.[3]

Decisions to boost children's knowledge of letters and sounds are made on the basis of knowing that there is a strong relationship between this knowledge and progress in beginning literacy instruction. For example, one of the strongest single predictors of early progress in reading and writing in English across countries is letter knowledge.[4] Consistent with this, differences on conventional school literacy measures, including letter knowledge, are apparent between Māori and Pacific Islands children in economically poorer schools and other children on entry to school. These children also score lower on a range of measures, such as concepts about print and other literacy-related measures.[5]

Progress in phonics – why not elsewhere?

One might think that, given the core programme and an increasing concern for promoting letter knowledge and understanding of relationships between letters and sounds, a balanced programme with successful outcomes for children would eventuate. But this has not been the case for these children. What is puzzling is that despite the children initially having lower scores in conventional literacy measures, the instruction available enables them to develop to nationally expected levels in letter knowledge and knowledge of letter–sound relationships. But this does not translate into generalised high levels of progress. Why is this?

The actual gaps and the risks for future learning

The situation is described in Table 1. It plots growth in some core reading and writing measures in a cross-section of these children on entry to school and after one year at school. It compares progress with national benchmarks on entry to school (where available) and at the end of the first year of instruction. The measures are concepts about print, letter identification, hearing and recording sounds, recognition of high-frequency words in the core reading series (WORD1), recognition of a more general set of words (WORD2), writing vocabulary, and text reading level after one year of instruction.[6] The averages for children at five years and six years are given.

Table 1

Growth in reading and writing on entry to school and to the end of one year at school (and benchmarks where available)

Task	Age Group			
	5.0-year-olds (N = 108)	*Benchmarks average*	*6.0-year-olds* (N = 100)	*Benchmarks middle range*
Concepts about print	5.3	9.5	13.2	14–16
Letter identification	10.5	21.7	43.7	44–49
Hearing and recording sounds	2.4	-	22.2	18–27
Word 1	0.4	0.7	7.4	10–12
Word 2	0.2	-	10.7	20+
Writing vocabulary	1.0	2.0	14.3	29–35
Text reading level	-	-	5.5	9

Concepts about print (Clay, 1993) has 24 graded items such as early conventions of directionality. Letter identification (Clay, 1993) uses a list of 54 letters (upper case and lower case and some alternative letter forms). Hearing and recording sounds (Clay, 1993) samples phonological knowledge with a total possible score of 37 phonemes heard. Writing vocabulary (Clay, 1993) records the number of words able to be written in ten minutes. Text level is the highest-level text able to be read in a graded series.

Adapted from Phillips, McNaughton & MacDonald (2001)

These children had very low scores on conventional literacy measures on entry to school. Not shown in this table are their scores on receptive and expressive English language assessments, which were also very low. However, despite low entry levels in their conventional literacy knowledge and in their receptive and expressive English-language skills, after twelve months of instruction, the children had made reasonable progress in three areas. Their knowledge of letters and their phonological knowledge were at the levels expected for six-year-old children in general classrooms. Their concepts of book language were within, or close to, expected levels.

Another way to show these outcomes after a year at school is to express them as a "risk" of not being at expected levels in these schools.[7] The risk is the relationship between the proportion of children expected to be at or above a certain benchmark (in this case, at or above stanine four) and the actual proportion of children at or above that benchmark.[8] In recognition of letters and in knowledge of sounds, the risk of not being at expected levels had disappeared by the time the children were six. For concepts about books and in core word recognition, there was almost a twofold risk of not being at or above the benchmarks. For not reading at text level, for writing vocabulary, and for generalised word recognition in English, there was a threefold to fivefold increase in risk.

Figure 3
Risk of not being at expected levels at 6.0 years [1.0 equals no risk]

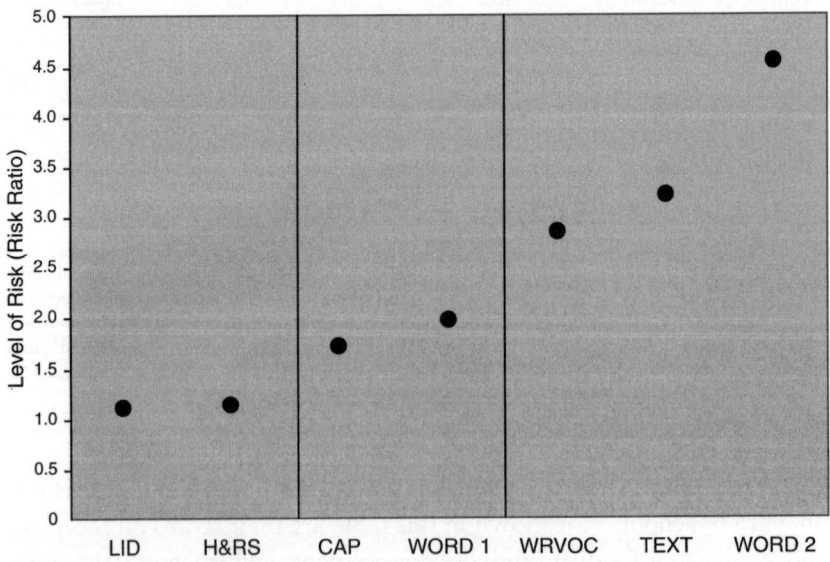

Adapted from Phillips, McNaughton and MacDonald (2001)

Low progress constraining further progress

The programme of instruction was sufficient for the components of letter identification and phonological knowledge as tapped by these measures after twelve months at school. However, by one year, these children's core sight word vocabulary was somewhat low, and it was particularly low for a wider, generalised group of words. Their basic writing vocabulary was low, too, and they were very different from groups of children in other schools in the level of texts that they could read. The implication is that instruction for extended word recognition, writing words, and text reading appears to be less effective in these schools than in others.

After several years of instruction, significant and substantial differences in literacy achievement have appeared between Māori and Pacific Islands children in schools serving economically poorer communities and other New Zealand children. The differences are particularly marked in reading comprehension and writing for a variety of purposes.[9] The beginnings of these differences can be seen in the profiles for the five- to six-year-old children described here, and the picture, like similar patterns elsewhere, is one of low levels of progress constraining further progress.[10]

Getting the balance right

From the findings of this study, we could infer that instruction that is particularly effective for developing decoding skills may not be effective for accelerating text-based reading and writing unless deliberate attempts to incorporate that knowledge into text reading and writing occur.[11] Instruction that enables children to integrate their knowledge of skills in the service of decoding, understanding, and producing texts is indicated.

The profiles of the Māori and Pacific Islands children described earlier altered substantially when literacy instruction focused more on the incorporation of relevant knowledge into text-based reading and writing. The overall programme is described in greater detail in Chapter 10. It was built around intensive teaching in the activities of reading to children, instructional reading, "interactive" writing, and "re-creative" writing. One feature of the programme was the deliberate enhancement of children's knowledge through "wordwork". In this activity, teachers and children worked with letters on whiteboards to incorporate knowledge explicitly as the need arose during instructional reading and interactive writing. The purpose was to make apparent to the children their existing knowledge of words and letters and the relevance of this knowledge to their text reading and text writing. But the "wordwork" was explicitly integrated into children's early reading of texts and their writing.

This explicit instruction, with the goal of building and incorporating knowledge, was part of a programme in which children reached near national expectations in their reading and writing by the end of their first year of schooling. The risk of their not being at expected levels had reduced markedly after the program (see Figure 4).

Figure 4

Risk of not being at expected levels at 6.0 years, after educational instruction [1.0 equals no risk]

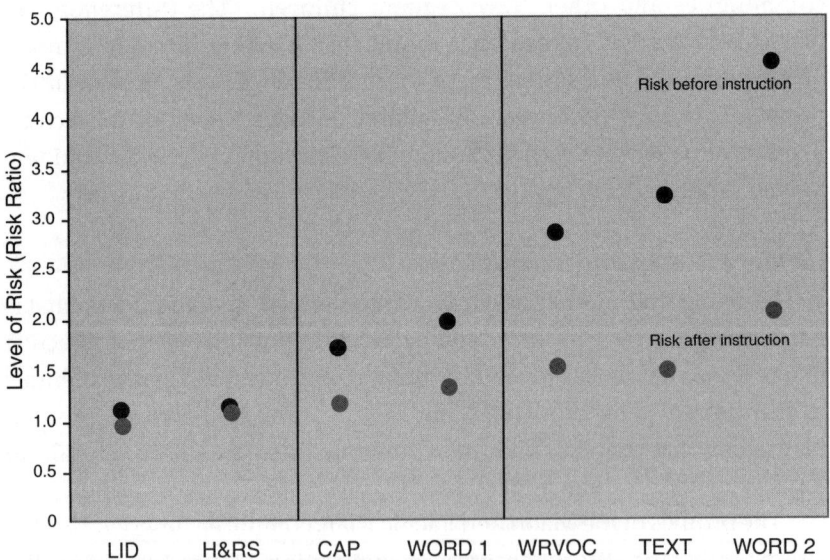

Adapted from Phillips, McNaughton and MacDonald (2001)

How balance can accommodate incorporation

These descriptions of classrooms and programmes point to what it means to achieve a balance in literacy instruction through incorporating children's knowledge of letters and sounds. But to understand in detail how this can happen effectively, we need a finer-grained analysis of what is involved in teaching, especially when teaching is referred to as being systematic and explicit.

What the teacher does

As they teach, teachers make particular statements, they direct, and they pose questions. These are the "teaching acts" that occur within activities in which teachers and learners engage. The dimension that features in all these teaching acts is their degree of explicitness. At one end of the range, teaching acts are more specific – what is expected to be learned and can be learned is made explicit. At the other end, they are more non-specific – what might be learned is implicit or embedded in the activity.[12] For our purposes here, we divide teaching acts on this dimension into two simple categories – explicit or implicit.

Teaching acts in phonics

The dimension of teaching acts involving phonics is whether these acts happen in relation to, or in isolation from, text. Here, "text" means a piece of connected, meaningful prose as distinct from an isolated decoding exercise.[13] We divide teaching acts on this dimension into two simple categories – text-free or text-connected.

Four types of teaching acts

We can put these two dimensions, with their simplified categories, into a matrix to give us a typology of four teaching acts. When we study what teachers do when they teach phonics, we can categorise their teaching acts relatively easily, given the following definitions:

- An "explicit" teaching act is one in which information about what is to be learned is provided verbally.
- A "text-connected" teaching act is one that focuses on a piece of connected meaningful prose.

Figure 5 shows what the matrix looks like and includes examples of beginning reading or writing activities that illustrate the four types of teaching acts. Text-connected teaching acts occur in versatile activities; for example, during guided reading. Text-free teaching acts occur in narrowly defined, and hence less versatile, activities.

Figure 5
Four types of teaching acts

	Text-free	**Text-connected**
Explicit	*Type 1 (examples)* • Instruct sounds from letters • Instruct letters from sounds	*Type 2 (examples)* • Feedback to oral reading error • Guided text editing – letters
Implicit	*Type 3 (examples)* • "IRE" sequence – flash cards • Dictation rhyming words	*Type 4 (examples)* • Model for word – reading • Model for word – writing

Type 1 "explicit/text-free" teaching acts

This type of teaching act is explicit teaching within an activity of limited versatility; for example, a complete exercise involving a specific instructional sequence for teaching vowel–consonant blends ("these two letters /c/ and /a/ say /kuh – a"). Relatively explicit information is given, and the focus is on the items and the knowledge associated with them in isolation. No reference is made to how those items might relate to a piece of connected text. An example from writing would be an instructional sequence that focuses on helping children to write letters corresponding to particular sounds – again, isolated from a piece of connected writing.

Type 2 "explicit/text-connected" teaching acts

This type of act is explicit teaching within an activity of high versatility. It might occur during guided reading; for example, when, on the basis of a child's miscue ("can" for "cat"), a teacher provides information about sounds that go to make up a word. The feedback (how to make the sounds "kuh – a – t") is explicit information (about letter–sound relationships) related to a piece of connected text. An example from a writing conference occurs when a teacher guides a child to write a word, sounding out the components as each letter is written. Again, an act of specific teaching occurs within a highly versatile activity in relation to a piece of connected text.

Type 3 "implicit/text-free" teaching acts

This type of act is implicit teaching within an activity of limited versatility. It might occur in an activity such as an "Initiation Response Evaluation" (IRE) dialogue sequence (Cazden, 1988). This comprises teacher Initiation ("What is this word?"), child Response ("It's cat"), and teacher Evaluation ("Yes"), using, for example, groups of rhyming words (cat, rat, hat). The sequence implicitly provides detectable patterns of sound–letter relationships, as would a sequence of rhyming words provided for written dictation. It is not, however, related to a piece of connected text.

Type 4 "implicit/text-connected" teaching acts

This type of act occurs in highly versatile activities but with little explicit guidance or intervention by the teacher. Reading and writing texts with their associated incidental word acquisition are examples of this. In the case of phonics, for example, the teacher may provide a model for saying or writing a word that occurs during a shared reading of a book or a shared writing activity. The information about letter–sound relationships is embedded in the whole model and not specifically taught.

Debating the systematic teaching of phonics

This typology helps us to understand how a balance that accommodates incorporation can take place. In this respect, it helps to clarify a confusion that has existed in debates about phonics teaching in New Zealand. The New Zealand version of the phonics debate centres on one question – do teachers of beginning reading and writing *systematically* teach knowledge and use of grapheme–phoneme relationships?

The protagonists on one side argue that teachers do not teach phonics. They point out that the curriculum guidelines for literacy instruction and educators' shared understanding about best practice restrict, if not exclude, direct phonics teaching. Children need to learn how to pronounce the sounds of isolated letters and overtly blend the subsyllabic sound units together. There are no specific exercises to guarantee the fulfilment of that need. Children may get some experience of this incidentally as they read texts, but that experience is insufficient, the argument runs, and is a prime cause for failing readers to fail.

Protagonists on the other side argue that when children are exposed to a text-oriented programme, they can work out and understand letter–sound relationships because the information is available embedded in the texts.[14] Incidental acquisition of this "item learning" is not only possible, but it should be the primary means for learning. If teachers deliberately use decoding exercises to teach phonics, the argument goes, they run the risk of diverting the child's attention away from real reading.

The debate, in fact, centres around confusion about what counts as systematic teaching. There is confusion, too, about the meaning of the terms "incidental teaching" and "incidental learning".

Confusing incidental teaching with unplanned teaching

Teaching acts that occur, as it were, on the run in text activities, particularly Type 2 (explicit/text-connected) teaching acts, are not necessarily unplanned when viewed in the light of teachers' major purposes. For example, teachers in New Zealand classrooms report an expectation that, in year one, children will be deliberately learning about spelling, vocabulary, word knowledge, and conventions in writing, more so than learning about forms and purposes of writing. A representative sample of thirty-five teachers in Auckland schools reported that, in their practices of writing and writing conferences, the conventions of writing and spelling, and awareness of these, were kept in the foreground (Glasswell, McNaughton, and Parr, 1993). Incidental should not be confused with unplanned and might better be reframed as contingent.

Confusion over incidental learning

A further confusion is between the concepts of incidental teaching and incidental learning. Incidental learning happens in complex learning tasks associated with the acquisition of knowledge that is difficult to make explicit (such as grammatical rules). Incidental learning is associated with opportunities to generalise and transfer skills. To reiterate points made in previous chapters, the potential for incidental learning is restricted in activities of limited versatility in which item-based teaching occurs. Conversely, this potential is enhanced in activities of high versatility.

This is where getting the balance is important to individual children. In some respects, there may be a trade-off between extensive use of Type 1 (explicit/text-free) teaching acts and incidental learning. While versatile activities enable incidental learning to occur, if children are not acquiring ample knowledge incidentally, they may need explicit teaching outside connected text, the benefit being that what needs to be learned is made more obvious.

Incorporating phonics in teaching children "at risk" in schools

This may help to explain the complicated situation that we have described in New Zealand schools. The confusions are reduced if one considers the presence of each of the four types of teaching acts in classrooms. Each type contributes in different ways to the needed development of phonological knowledge and phonemic awareness.

Generally speaking, children in the first years of literacy instruction rapidly reach the ceiling in a range of phonological measures, showing that they have acquired extensive and detailed knowledge of phonology and its uses.[15] This rapid acquisition happens within a programme that may not deliberately foster this sort of knowledge outside the use of connected text. However, the rates of gain and the extent of the knowledge indicate that significant learning occurs – from the various types of teaching acts, through incidental learning, and through a combination of both. The typology indicates those sources of explicit teaching that might contribute to this learning. As we noted earlier, research in New Zealand classrooms suggests the frequent presence of Type 2 (explicit/text-connected) teaching acts with some Type 1 (explicit/text-free) acts; hence, the programme does not restrict this learning.

This phenomenon is not limited to New Zealand classrooms, as some intensive studies of children's instruction in both "skills-based" and "whole language" classrooms in the United States have shown.[16] An analysis of the acquisition of alphabetic knowledge over the first two years of school, in both kinds of programmes, indicates similar degrees of learning. Much of the instruction in the "whole language" classrooms would be categorised as implicit, although explicit phonics instruction was provided in both settings, albeit through different kinds of activities.

So why has this general approach to the acquisition of literacy not been as effective for children from diverse cultural and language backgrounds? The specific phonological skills that these children need are no different from those that other children need.

Knowing where the children are at

Our argument is that teachers, on the whole, know less about these particular children's expertise in literacy and language and are less able to identify relevant knowledge and incorporate that knowledge into text reading and writing. The emergent understanding of written language that these children bring to school is less likely to be recognised by teachers, especially if this understanding is embedded in everyday family activities. This is as true for children's knowledge of letters and letter–sound relationships (for example, embedded in their being able to write their names) as it is for their knowledge of books and their purposes (for example, embedded in listening to Bible stories).

A telling illustration of this situation can be found in a study of the development of children's writing both before school, in family activities, and over the first months at school (Goodridge, 1995). The seventeen children came from Māori, Pākehā, and Sāmoan families. All the children had been involved in a range of family writing activities before they came to school, and could write some or all of their names. Guidance for writing some letters of the alphabet had occurred in all families. Other writing activities took place with interested and helpful family members, who often acted as scribes for what the children wanted to write.

One Māori child was fascinated with new cars and drew and labelled them; for example, identifying one as a Feroza by personally writing FOZE (the Z being written in mirror image). A Sāmoan child was fascinated by TV programmes about mutants and transformers. He composed letters to a friend and told stories about these transformers, which he attempted to write, in one example using the letters B, E, G, H, T, and G.

Their teachers generally believed that these children knew very little about literacy. They gave them opportunities to write texts during writing sessions, often not knowing about the topics (and the family writing activities) that were familiar to the children, and they did not know, and could not therefore identify, the nascent knowledge that the children had. They took few opportunities to identify the children's existing knowledge of letters and sounds and incorporate this into activities.

Getting all the evidence about what children need

This discussion has highlighted some weaknesses in the ways we have used research information to inform effective instruction. Claims have often been made about what children need without considering all the appropriate information. Planning effective teaching of skills such as phonics for these children should include detailed knowledge of how their literacy develops and under what instructional conditions. When developmental profiles such as those described here are tied to specified instructional conditions, they provide important pieces of information.

Limitations in predicting development in literacy

We rely, often quite heavily, on known relationships between early knowledge and later development (for example, the significant predictive power of alphabet knowledge) to make judgements about the needs of linguistically and culturally diverse children. Research that shows how early differences between learners correlate with their later achievement provides some guidance, but it has several limitations.

One is that certain features of development can be different under different programmes of instruction. For example, rates, levels, and features of words recognised are all likely to vary according to the pattern of instruction, including the texts used over the first year of instruction. So it is important to analyse profiles in particular instructional contexts.[17]

Another limitation is that early differences that predict later differences cannot be said with certainty to cause them. This is not just a problem with the type of evidence. The research itself may be limited by the features of the skills it covers – it may not include all those features that might be associated with later achievement. For example, some recent studies that predict reading progress have not included early measures of writing skills. When measures of emergent writing are added into the research picture, they turn out to be significant predictors also.

The profiles described earlier also show that particular knowledge such as phonological knowledge and phonemic awareness, while necessary for the development of conventional classroom literacy, are not sufficient to guarantee generalised progress. Ignoring these limitations can lead to the adoption of "inoculation" models of children's development, where a dose of instruction is assumed to guarantee immunity to low levels of progress. Well-informed decisions are needed for children of diverse backgrounds who are at risk in schools.

The potential to confuse children

Teaching that employs text-based approaches and the flexible use of different types of teaching acts can be associated with progress across a broad range of literacy outcomes. However, just as there are dangers with an over-reliance on explicit types of teaching acts (Types 1 and 3), there is a potential for children's confusion from an overemphasis on implicit types of teaching acts (Types 2 and 4). Too much reliance on these might unwittingly discriminate against the very children for whom mainstream schools pose a risk.

This danger has been identified by both Delpit (1995) and Dyson (1999a), who emphasise different ways of overcoming the problem. Both argue that some approaches to reading (some forms of "whole language") and writing (some forms of "process writing") that advocate immersion are based on the assumption that there is a single developmental sequence associated with development and that children will spontaneously engage in the construction of needed knowledge and skills. If they do not, some proponents of the approaches argue, then the children are deficient or have inadequate skills, but direct teaching will stultify their capacity for problem solving and construction.

Giving children what they need

This illustrates a confusion over the role of explicitly teaching skills in instructional approaches that are concerned with meaning and promoting children's own authentic voices. The assumption that the same teaching approaches are appropriate for all children effectively shuts out children of diverse cultures and languages. In this way, *not* teaching skills, which might be rationalised as progressive and liberal, inadvertently maintains a culture of power that denies the students access to the skills that they need to unlock meanings – from basic elements of decoding and encoding to the discourse structures of classrooms. Even more importantly, staunch advocates of these approaches may shut out other (non-mainstream) educators' voices from effective debate, as Delpit argues:

> *Maybe, just maybe, these writing process teachers are so adamant about developing fluency because they have not really had the opportunity to realize the fluency the kids already possess. They hear only silence, they see only immobile pencils. And maybe the black teachers are so adamant against what they*

understand to be the writing process approach because they hear their students'
voices and see their fluency clearly .... [M]any supporters of the [writing process]
approach do indeed concern themselves with the technicalities of writing in their
own classrooms. However, writing process advocates often give the impression
that they view the direct teaching of skills to be restrictive to the writing process
at best, and at worst, politically repressive to students already oppressed by a
racist educational system. Black teachers, on the other hand, see the teaching of
skills to be essential to their students' survival. (Delpit, 1995, pages 17–18)

For Delpit, the concern is the availability of direct and explicit teaching but within the context of critical and creative thinking. For Dyson, it is also the provision of curriculum space and active guidance so that children's "multiple voices" are recognised and can be heard. Delpit provides evidence that mini-lessons in skills (direct instruction on writing conventions) in process-oriented classrooms, together with student-centred conferences, can be associated with positive changes in students' writing. This is, in part, the conclusion we have come to here. Teachers need to know what children currently know, both in the forms embedded in familiar activities outside of school and in those recognised in assessments for conventional literacy. Then they need to show to the children the relevance of that knowledge, incorporating it into versatile activities of text reading and writing.

Achieving a balance

The issue we have discussed in this chapter is not whether phonics is important. Clearly, it is essential that children develop phonological knowledge and awareness of sounds and letters early on in instruction. Rather, the issue is how best to teach the children for whom schools are a risky business and in ways that enable development in text reading and writing to be enhanced. Incorporation strategies can be found here, and there is evidence for their significance. But we argue that this is in the context of a flexible use of different types of teaching acts, exploiting the versatility that text-based activities offer. What does this imply about the knowledge and skills that teachers need? It is to this question that we now turn.

End Notes

1   See studies by Dahl, Scharer, Lawson, and Grogan (1999), and Fisher, Lapp, and Flood (1999).

2   See McNaughton (1999b).

3   See Timplerley, Robinson, and Bullard (1999), who describe the addition of programmes but who also note that, in many instances, this has occurred without knowing what children typically learn in the core programme or whether the add-on instruction contributes to generalised progress.

4   Arguments for more explicit teaching of phonemic awareness and alphabetic understanding specifically for linguistically and culturally diverse children have been made by Kame'enui and Carnine (1998) and Nicholson (1997).

5   The national data from School Entry Assessment show significant differences on measures of concepts about print and story retelling (Gilmore, 1998). Other studies indicate differences on measures of alphabet knowledge and writing vocabulary, although, when family literacy activities are described, it is apparent that children's preschool environments contain rich literacy experiences, albeit not necessarily well-matched with conventional school activities (McNaughton, 1995).

6   Measures of text reading are important because they reflect patterns of learning and teaching very directly. Progress on texts is particularly sensitive to teachers' skills for building on children's diverse knowledge – an area in which children in economically poor schools are very vulnerable (McNaughton, MacDonald, and Phillips, 2000). Low levels of progress in reading texts (and in writing words) is particularly significant because it severely restricts the opportunities for teaching and learning comprehension strategies and accumulating reading and writing vocabularies. It also restricts the mutual facilitation between a child's oral and written lexicon (Biemiller, 1999; Stanovich, Cunningham, and West, 1999).

7   The idea of risk here is the same as that described in Chapter 1. It is of schools being risky places for some children, in this case, to a measurable degree.

8   The benchmark used is one commonly used by teachers in New Zealand. Progress is compared with a normalised distribution of 9 levels (stanines). Scores at stanine 4 or above represent 77 percent of the normal distribution, while scores below stanine 4 would be in the bottom 23 percent of the distribution. Risk is calculated by dividing the expected proportion of children being at or above the benchmark (that is, 0.77) with the proportion of children actually above. A risk of 1.00 means that the proportions are the same. The higher the risk, the fewer the number of children at or above the benchmark. For example, a risk factor of 4.0 means that only about 19 percent of the children are at or above the benchmark.

9   See Flockton and Crooks (1997; 1999; 2001), Wagemaker (1992), Wilkinson (1998), and Wylie, Thompson, and Lythe (1999).

10 This picture of early low levels of progress constraining further progress is consistent with longitudinal studies of groups of children in the United States that have initial disparities, which remain after four years (Juel, 1994; Stanovich, 1986). The disparities on more general measures of text reading and writing tend to increase (McNaughton, 1995; Nicholson, 1997), a finding that is consistent with those of other researchers on early patterns of low progress elsewhere (Juel, 1994; Stanovich, 1986).

11 The most extensively quoted and persuasive of these studies, reported by Foorman, Francis, Fletcher, Schatschneider, and Mehta (1998), is now one of several experimental

studies of programmes that emphasise systematic and explicit phonics instruction in the early grades for children in schools serving minority children in poor communities. There is consensus across these studies. They produce limited transfer to comprehension and real text reading and writing, outcomes commented on not only in experimental research but also in other descriptive and ethnographic studies (Allington and Woodside-Jones,1999; Dyson, 1999a; Ladson-Billings, 1994; Nicholson, 1997; Taylor, Anderson, Au, and Raphael, 2000).

12 Cazden (1993) introduced this dimension and refers to points along it as "telling", "revealing", and "immersing". See also McNaughton (1995).

13 The recent distinction between decodable texts and meaningful texts draws attention to this complexity (Heibert and Martin, 2001; Snow, Burns, and Griffin, 1998).

14 For instruction in New Zealand, further discussion of the first of these positions can be found in Tunmer and Chapman (1997), Tunmer, Chapman, Prochnow, and Ryan (1998), Nicholson (1992), and Nicholson and Galliene (1995); and of the second position in Emmett, Pollock, and Limbrick (1996) and Smith and Elley (1994).

15 In addition to the information from the profile descriptions, Tunmer, Chapman, Prochow, and Ryan (1997) have found that children making typical progress acquire extensive knowledge with measures such as phoneme deletion (where an initial consonant segment is deleted and the task is to say the remaining segment, such as ice from mice) and onset and rhyme sensitivity (where children have to judge which two of three orally presented words sound the same, such as *sail, nail, boot* or *hair, pin, pig*).

16 Similar conclusions were reached by McIntyre and Freppon (1994).

17 This is partly an issue of ecological validity (Bronfenbrenner, 1979) as well as a theoretically driven need to analyse contexts because development is a product of social and individual forces (McNaughton, 1999a).

Chapter 5

Being an Expert

Overview of the chapter

Expert awareness and effectiveness

One of the dilemmas mentioned in Chapter 2 was that the more open and versatile the activities that the teacher uses, the greater the potential for confusion, ambiguity, and a lack of common understanding between teacher and learner. Part of the solution to this dilemma lies in teachers' awareness. In relation to the learner, they need to be aware of both the instructional focus of activities and where the learner is at. They also need to be aware of where they themselves are at – what they know, value, and act on.

What does it take for a teacher to make effective connections with linguistically and culturally diverse learners, to help them build on the familiar in the ways that we have been discussing in the previous two chapters? To answer this question, we need first to discuss what it means to be a teacher. Then we look at answers to the question as they relate to the individual student – a daunting task in itself. In the latter part of the chapter, we look at answers as they relate to what a teacher can achieve in a classroom of, maybe, thirty individuals – even more of a challenge.

The teacher as a professional expert

What does it mean to be a teacher? From our point of view here, it means to be an expert in a profession – in the case of a teacher, someone who is engaged in the task of deliberately co-constructing someone else's expertise. Teachers become experts in the professional community of teachers. Their expertise, like other forms of expertise, lies in acquiring knowledge about what they do, devising strategies for meeting goals, and developing ways of reflecting on and regulating their performance. Their expertise is explicit, made so through deliberate training. From that initial training, and beyond it, they acquire tools, such as a technical language or an explicit curriculum that specifies what is valued and what is expected, that enable them to broaden and deepen their effectiveness.

The expert ideas, strategies, and skills that teachers use come from a wide range of sources. They are dynamic – partly acquired during initial training but continuing to develop through teachers' professional lives. Some come from explicit instruction, through deliberate professional training. But many are acquired, practised, and modified in everyday classrooms and school settings, with teachers learning, like apprentices, through participation in the practices of their professional communities.[1]

Teachers' ideas

Part of teachers' expertise is the variety of ideas that they have about the nature of children's development and appropriate forms of teaching and learning. The ideas include beliefs about what are appropriate goals for and stages in children's development. Teachers' ideas bear directly on the quality of connections that teachers can make with learners.

Recently, there has been a resurgence of interest by educational researchers in the ideas that teachers have about teaching and learning. Olson and Bruner (1996) claim that knowing about these ideas and intentions enables us to account better for what, and how, teaching and learning happen in classrooms. This is part of the view, discussed in Chapter 1, that both teachers and learners bring ideas and intentions to classroom activities and that these ideas and intentions create channels for teaching and learning.

The influence of frameworks of ideas

Researchers have distinguished several overarching frameworks or "folk pedagogies" held by teachers. These reflect the major traditions of thinking on the nature of learning and of children's development.[2] Our interest here is in how these frameworks influence ideas held about specific curriculum domains, such as early literacy and beginning literacy instruction. For example, with a constructivist framework of ideas, teachers tend to think that the development of literacy follows a predictable and uniform sequence because processes inherent within the child direct the acquisition of literacy (see, for example, Goodman, 1990). With a sociocultural framework, such as that adopted in this book, teachers tend to think that literacy development can take many pathways, paralleling the varieties of guidance and expertise found in different communities, including those of schools.

The frameworks set parameters for, and constrain, what counts for their holders as significant knowledge. For example, a constructivist viewpoint focuses on knowledge specified by a predictable developmental sequence. A sociocultural viewpoint focuses on knowledge that arises from activities in particular contexts of use.

The variety of teachers' ideas about children's development means that teachers are likely to differ widely in what counts for them as children's literacy. That difference could range from only taking account of features directly associated with conventional school literacy, through to including family and community literacy practices in the frame of reference.

The literacy funnel

The influence of teachers' frameworks of ideas on their teaching of literacy is demonstrated dramatically in a study of teachers' responses to children's writing on entry to school (Goodridge, 1998). The study involved children from Māori, Sāmoan, and Pākehā families in low-income and low-employment urban communities in New Zealand. It included the children's writing during the six months before entry to school as well as during the period of transition after entry. The schools invited families to bring examples and descriptions of children's writing that came from family activities during the six months before entry.

These portfolios of family writing included children's personal or joint productions (in which they did not necessarily complete the written product). As with families in other countries, activities that had writing a name as a product were common. But, as research has shown, a wide variety of other writing activities can occur in families (Heath, 1983), and this was true of these families, including forms of expository writing and of making messages. The patterns of activity varied considerably. A few families were focused on name writing, letters of the alphabet, and little else. In most families, children were developing writing within several different activities – making messages, narratives, and expositions as well as names and letters. As children approached entry to school, the patterns varied further, with parents often anticipating what children might need to know and be able to do when they got to school, such as being able to write on a line or write with capitals.

When a child entered school, the parents shared the child's portfolio of emergent writing with the new teacher. The researcher had assumed that this sharing of writing activities that the child had experienced and performed in some way would lead the teacher to use the activities systematically within writing lessons. These familiar activities, however, although appreciated by the teachers, had little impact on the ways in which the teachers interacted with the children as new entrants.

Figure 6
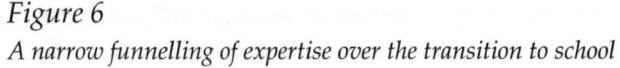
A narrow funnelling of expertise over the transition to school

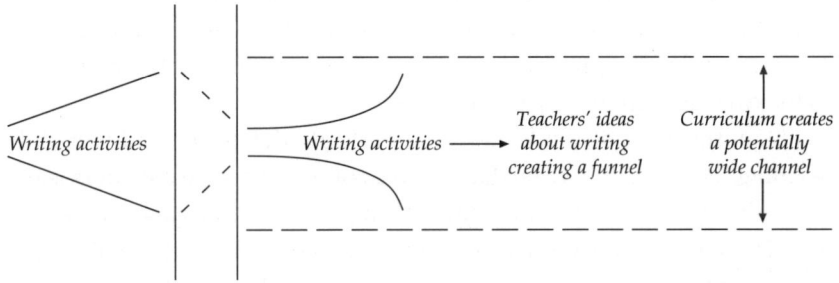

Before school (widening expertise)   At school (initial narrowing of expertise)

Reproduced by permission of Heinemann, from Stirring the Waters: The Influence of Marie Clay, edited by J.S. Gaffney and B.J. Askew.

The findings of this research are depicted in Figure 6. Children's increasing range of activities and emergent expertise is shown on the left-hand side of the diagram. In the middle is the transition to school. At the right is the curriculum potential for types of writing to be developed further, which is relatively wide in New Zealand. Within this is the teachers' narrower focus as it often operates in beginning instruction. In this study, it was initially limited to forms of personal narrative occasioned by the invitation to write "a story".

The diagram graphically represents a kind of "funnel" hypothesis, in this case, applied to the development of writing over the transition to school. That is, teachers' beliefs about what counts as reading or writing or appropriate forms of expertise create a funnel (what they are able to "see" and respond to) through which the diverse forms of literacy have to pass.

Wide curriculum, narrow delivery

The English curriculum in New Zealand (Ministry of Education, 1994) allows teachers to identify and respond to a wide variety of forms of language and literacy. But the activities selected, arranged, and deployed by teachers working with beginning children may deliver a curriculum that narrows, rather than broadens, a child's emergent expertise. For example, modelling, conferencing, and other activities associated with the question "What is your story?" convey a message that narrative in general, and personal recount in particular, is the primary way to write or, at least, the building block to other ways of writing. Thus, in the case of writing, teachers' beliefs about the priority of narrative (and personal recount), and the appropriate instruction for it, might limit their response to the diversity offered by the learners.

Now this may be (and often is) a perfectly defensible and workable teaching decision. It may be that to have children become narrators is the most effective way to promote the learning of basic skills and to provide a bridge to other forms of writing. Such immediacy and personalising of meaning forms a powerful basis for instruction. Also, written narratives offer the potential for teacher and learner to establish shared understandings and utilise personal and culturally relevant topics, as we have shown in previous chapters. Indeed, instructional activities involving narrative offer the kind of wide channels within which personal expertise is more likely to be seen.

However, narrative may not be the only, or the best, way into the wide channel for every student. There is a need for adaptability and diversity here, too. The curriculum and its associated tools may create the space for this diversity. But teachers' ideas and practices may get in the way of taking advantage of it.

Expert awareness of diversity in individuals

Children take a big step in developing their expertise when they become aware of what they are doing as they learn. This principle of awareness can also be applied to teachers' expertise and its development (Sternberg, 1998). In the case of literacy, teachers bring to instructional encounters a set of ideas about the nature of literacy and the possible diversity of forms that literacy expertise can take. This can be regarded as their general awareness of diversity in literacy.

The level of their awareness of diversity is reflected in how much teachers know (and do not know) about individual children's expertise in literacy, including forms and functions based in the children's families and community. Teachers' ability to develop an expert level of this awareness depends on their understanding literacy as a variety of forms of expertise that are co-constructed through social practices – that is, that the processes of learning and teaching literacy, and the forms of expertise in it, are reflections of the social and cultural identities of the participants.

Awareness of literacy diversity at the beginning of school

Referring to teachers' ideas about beginning school literacy in terms of awareness rather than knowledge enables us to emphasise how knowledge might be applied and developed. For example, what potential does a teacher's understanding and perception of children's literacy development have for applying their ideas on literacy instruction to individual learners and for personalising that knowledge? We assume that it is not sufficient to know that knowledge of the alphabet, or letter–sound relationships, or text types feature in children's literacy. It is also important to know how these features may or may not apply to individual new entrants. Moreover, the term "awareness" includes the idea that one knows the status of one's own knowledge. And the presence of this awareness leads to a further assumption – that teachers' ideas are dynamic and can be modified by reflection on their interactions with learners.

Focusing on awareness of diversity provides a way of connecting a teacher's ideas about children's literacy development to the specific actions that they take to gain personalised knowledge about each student.

Levels of awareness of diversity

What does teachers' general awareness of literacy diversity look like in schools serving children with diverse language and cultural identities from economically poorer communities? This question was explored with a group of twenty teachers in such schools in New Zealand, including three Māori and four Pacific Islands teachers.[3] Most had been teaching for five or more years and had basic teaching qualifications. We asked them, "In what ways can children differ in their emergent literacy?" and "Describe the possible range of strengths that five-year-old children bring to your school in their emergent literacy" (from their family/early childhood experiences). They then chose a new entrant and provided a specific description of these attributes.

The teachers differed markedly in the kinds of things that they looked for in a new entrant to establish where that child was at. However, the most striking feature of the responses was that they seldom referred to possible variations in children's skills that might develop through family literacy activities. This was despite the teachers coming from a range of cultural and language groups, and some of them being members of the same cultural communities as the children. For example, the teachers could have referred to how many families in these communities read Bible stories to children in family devotions or how children develop expertise in the recitation of texts. Rather, they focused almost exclusively on descriptions of school-related knowledge, strategies, and skills.

Within this focus, the teachers did vary in what they looked for. One teacher could see a wide potential range in markers of conventional school literacy:

> *... from little knowledge of books, words letters etc. ... to already reading or attempting to; to being able to stay on task for a limited time to being interested in the length of a whole text; some focus on pictures and prefer their own text (invented), some taking time to realise pictures and text combine for meaning, some to learn that text is constant. In writing, from not being able to hold a pencil [and] make a recognisable mark to being able to draw a detailed picture, dictate a relevant text and/or draw a detailed picture.*

Possible strengths in a group of students were identified as:

> *Knowledge of early book skills ie L > R, 1:1 [sic], print contains a message that is constant, ideas can be conveyed in print and read as written. Recognition of symbols eg M (McDonalds), alphabet – recitation and or recognition. Recognise their name, write it, experiences and vocabulary they can relate to literacy.* (Teacher 1)

Other teachers had a narrower range:

> *Some can't write names others can. Some can't point and read others only talk about the pictures. Some scribble others can draw pictures.*

Children's potential strengths were identified as:

> *Can write own name. Can talk about pictures. Learn ABC.* (Teacher 2)

Typically, the more extensive descriptions of potential diversity were associated with a similar degree of differentiated knowledge of a target child. When asked to describe a particular child, the two teachers reported above wrote the following.

Child 'x' has ...

Familiarity with books, willingness to "read", some alphabet recognition and sounds to match, early book skills and attempting 1:1 reading, regular return of home reader, fluency in Sāmoan and a knowledge of English with some good vocabulary. Could write his name recognisably, hold a pencil correctly, use space effectively, draw detailed "story" and attempted to write his own story, hear sounds in words and give letters for some though not able to write them yet with confidence, dictate different texts to different pictures outside formula ("I went to ... or I am ..."). (Teacher 1)

Pre reading, pre writing. (Teacher 2)

When family literacy events were identified, these were primarily those book experiences that are often associated with mainstream family practices. Teachers noted that children could differ in terms of:

Language needs, whether they are read to or talked to, if they have been "introduced" to books / print. (Teacher 3)

Specific children's strengths were then tied to storybook experience:

Awareness that print has meaning. (Teacher 4) *(Phillips, McNaughton and MacDonald, 2001, pages 157 – 158)*

These comments show how the teachers had differing concepts about literacy and the skills, situated in particular activities, that children have learned. From these concepts, a teacher knows the dimensions along which one child in a class might differ from another. At their most inclusive, these dimensions would encompass children's experiences in social and cultural practices as well as aspects of conventional literacy.

Diversity in literacy expertise among new entrants

At the same time as the teachers' awareness of diversity was being probed, the conventional literacy knowledge of 111 Māori and Pacific Islands five-year-olds entering the teachers' schools was being investigated. The descriptions of these children showed a considerable range of scores in markers of conventional literacy (see Table 2). For example, the average child had just over five concepts about print, but the variability was almost four concepts – meaning that it was not uncommon for children to arrive at school with up to nine concepts or with none. Letter identification had a similar pattern, as did phonological knowledge. The children could write, on average, one word (usually their name), but two to three words were common.

Two measures of (English) language competency are shown, too. One, a story retelling task, provides a profile on several dimensions, including listening comprehension, sentence and vocabulary use, and the organisation and expressiveness of their retold stories. The average score (out of a total of eighteen) indicates an ability to tell stories with some understanding and clarity, and the spread of scores shows a wide range of performance. The measure of receptive vocabulary has a similar pattern.

Table 2

Children's scores on conventional literacy and language tasks on entry to school

Task	Average	Standard deviation
Concepts about print	5.3	3.7
Letter identification	10.5	14.9
Hearing and recording sounds	2.5	4.3
Writing vocabulary	1.0	2.4
Story retelling	9.3	3.8
Receptive vocabulary	31.2	19.9

Writing vocabulary (Clay, 1993) records the number of words able to be written in 10 minutes. Story retelling – Tell me/Ki Mai (Learning Media, 1997) – has 6 dimensions, each with a 3-point scale. Receptive vocabulary assesses children's receptive (picture) language (PPVT – Dunn & Dunn, 1997).

Adapted from Phillips, McNaughton & MacDonald (2001)

The descriptions show that, on arrival at school, the children had developed a considerable range of conventional literacy knowledge and skills in English. (More than half had a home language other than English.) So, it would be appropriate for teachers to see these children as already having a reasonable base of conventional literacy knowledge generally, but they could expect considerable differences between children. They could also expect individual children to differ in their patterns of knowledge across these tasks. Most importantly, perhaps, they could expect that the children would have an extra set of resources – their familiarity with home and community literacy practices – which would not show up in these scores.

Along with their expectations of variations in these dimensions of literacy, teachers could also expect diversity within community groups. For example, because a child comes from a Pākehā or Sāmoan family, the child might be expected, initially but not necessarily, to be familiar with core Pākehā or Sāmoan literacy practices. In the various ranges of literacy activities and values, children *within* a cultural or social group can differ significantly, just as much as social and cultural groups can differ from one another.

So, in relation to our discussion of teachers' expertise, awareness of diversity refers to teachers' awareness of the possible scope of children's experience and performance of literacy and language activities on entry to school. The level of this awareness is reflected in their practices for finding out about an individual child's strengths.

The significance of teachers' awareness

While there is a complicated relationship between teachers' ideas and their practices, one would expect that what a teacher knew about children's literacy would somehow influence the ways in which they taught. There is compelling evidence for how significant a teacher's knowledge of children can be for effective literacy instruction. One example comes from a re-analysis of the New Zealand data in the 1990 International Educational Achievement study. This had shown that there were large gaps in reading achievement after four years at school between children who had English as a first language and those who did not. When the data was re-analysed, taking various factors into account, it was found that the gaps were smallest in classrooms where teachers had more extensive knowledge (gained through monitoring and assessment) of children's skills.[4]

Studies such as this provide general support for the ongoing gathering of detailed information about children's development in classroom learning, but they do not directly test our concern in this chapter – how a teacher's level of awareness of diversity is significant to their strategies for building on the familiar. There is both negative and positive evidence specifically for this.

The effects of knowing little about learners

Negative effects on children's learning are discernible when teachers lack awareness of diverse forms of language and literacy. Sometimes this can come from the teacher not sharing the same cultural background as the children. For example, Cazden (1988) describes classroom studies of two styles of oral narrative in first graders – those of European American and African American children. The "topic-centred" style of the European American children's narratives typically had a single topic. They were told in a linear fashion in a single timeframe and contained a resolution. The "episodic" style of the African American children typically contained a series of episodes linked, often implicitly, to some theme or person and with changing timeframes. The children's European American teacher could help to develop the topic-centred narratives but had difficulties extending the episodic narratives.

The episodic narratives were subsequently evaluated by both African American and European American teachers, and their evaluations were compared. African American teachers could understand the narratives and rated them more highly than European American teachers. When asked to assess the likelihood of the children's educational success, the former teachers were more positive than the latter.

However, while membership of the same cultural group as the children may assist a teacher's awareness, it does not guarantee that the children's expertise will be valued or incorporated and built on. Similarly, teachers who are not from the same cultural group can still achieve a degree of awareness through familiarity with children's cultural and language practices. Indeed, Cazden repeated her study in New Zealand and found that Anglo-European teachers there saw qualities in the episodic narratives that their counterparts in the United States were not able to see. And Ladson-Billings (1994) identified both African American and non-African American teachers as effective with African American students.

It is relatively easy to show that a teacher can create confusion through limited awareness of the language and literacy expertise of children. The teacher in the study reported by Cazden (1988) mistimed questions and cut episodic narratives off. Various other studies have shown teachers seeing the regular variations in pronunciation and syntax in Black English as mistakes and correcting them, with predictably negative outcomes.[5]

The effects of greater awareness

A large amount of research supports the general principle that academic achievement is related to teachers' ability to build on learners' experiences and frames of reference (Darling-Hammond, 1997). Some of that research was described in Chapter 3. A further example is the study of 140 classrooms (Knapp, Shields, and Turnbull, 1995) in schools serving economically poor communities that had attained better-than-average performance on conventional measures of reading and writing. Students learned most from teachers who took steps to connect learning to students' backgrounds. These teachers knew the children's knowledge base and connected their instruction more closely to children's home experiences.

John Hattie (1999), in a meta-analysis of a database of 180 000 studies representing over fifty million students, ranked the level of effect that instructional events had for enhancing student achievement. The most powerful event across these studies was feedback – providing information on how and what a child understands and misunderstands and what directions the child must take to improve. To do this, a teacher needs to know what the child currently knows. In the context of beginning literacy instruction, we have argued that this in turn is based on an awareness of the diversity of forms that children's literacy might take.

Clearly, belonging to the same cultural and language group as a child is neither sufficient in itself, nor necessary, to guarantee this awareness. Certainly, it may increase the potential to be aware. However, the research suggests that teachers who do not belong to their students' cultural group can nevertheless develop knowledge of it and a (bi-)cultural identity. The teachers that Ladson-Billings described as effective with African American children had various distinctive characteristics, one of which was a grounding in community patterns of language use.

Expert awareness of diversity in the classroom
The challenge of personalising instruction

How can a teacher, with maybe thirty children of diverse cultural and language backgrounds in the classroom, hope to know about the literacy experiences that each child brings? How do they get the knowledge that they need? This is a daunting challenge in the meeting of minds – teaching in circumstances where, on average, teachers are only able fleetingly to interact with children, providing a small dose of personalised feedback, possibly only a few seconds per day. There are three routes into this, none of them easy, but each one is utilised by expert teachers.

Children as informants

Effective teachers use both formal and informal ways of assessing and monitoring children to acquire the knowledge that they need to make expert instructional decisions. They know a lot about their children. This is true for all such teachers, irrespective of the classroom and the types of students. But here we are concerned with what effective teachers in diverse urban schools might do to build on what these children bring to school – in addition to what can be measured in conventional indicators of literacy.

One of the routes is provided by the kinds of highly versatile activities in which children are able to inject more of themselves and through which teachers are able to learn more about children's backgrounds, their skills, and their interests. We have argued above that teachers with a heightened awareness of diversity will be predisposed to look for patterns of diversity. Armed with this general approach, a teacher can construct an understanding of the child that is personalised by the child's contributions.

This is why writers such as Dyson express confidence that children's "cultural landscapes" and voices can be heard if teachers expect and allow them to present, elaborate, and explain their work and support them in doing so.[6] There is, of course, a management as well as an awareness issue here – to organise activities that enable children's voices to be heard and to manage the classroom so that all members of the class can engage in these activities as much as possible (Darling-Hammond, 1997). A child receiving a few seconds per day of personalised feedback is the all-too-familiar situation, reflecting the challenges of managing class engagement, as well as the expertise of the teacher to create extended interactions.

Researchers have described a number of facets of classroom organisation that can contribute to personalising interactions. One study (Wilkinson and Townsend, 2000) showed how an effective teacher in a school serving the economically poorest Māori and Pacific Islands communities in New Zealand used ability grouping effectively to identify the strengths of new entrants. There are problems associated with ability grouping, especially for students from cultural and language minorities, but these researchers report on a teacher who used such a grouping with greater flexibility than reported in other settings, thereby avoiding some of the problems associated with children being stuck on a low-level progress track.

The teacher in this study adopted a developmental emphasis in her grouping, focusing on fostering independent reading strategies and skills and having high expectations (see Chapter 10) for all students. She ensured that readers and texts were closely matched by choosing texts that fitted the readers' background knowledge in difficulty and language. This was based on a detailed knowledge of the books and of her students. The teacher continually looked for opportunities to move students up a gradient of difficulty with these books.

Groups were just one organisational structure. The teacher also used individual, paired, and whole-class approaches. She described a strategy of "roaming around" that she had adapted from the Reading Recovery intervention procedures (Clay, 1993). She let new entrant children attach to whichever reading groups they chose, drawing on the support of the older children in the community that she had created. In this way, she gave the new entrants opportunities to show what literacy behaviours they had.

On the first day, I let Olivia do what she wanted to and she just pottered around, tending to go toward what the other children were doing. See, not branching off on her own at all. On the second day, I found out that she's actually got quite good pencil handling skills. She knows how to work pencil and paper and make letter-like marks on the paper. She can't write her name but she can recognise it. She can talk all about pictures in a book. All these came up on the second day when I started to invite her to come with the Emergent group, when I was working with them ....

[O]ver that first week I would have seen if she could point words. Like I said, I found out within the first couple of days that she could talk about pictures. I can't remember exactly which day now. I would assume that if she could point words, which some New Entrants can .... [S]he couldn't [one-to-one point], she has absolutely no idea. I don't think she's even aware of the text being there yet. She's still looking at the pictures ... [I picked this up] in the group situation with her sitting next to me. (Wilkinson and Townsend, 2000, page 464)

Although this description mostly focuses on conventional markers of school literacy, the procedure adapted from Reading Recovery may provide a useful way of looking at the teaching acts required. In Reading Recovery, "roaming around in the known" is the term used for an initial period of time when the teacher attempts to find tasks and texts that enable the child and teacher to develop common understanding, common goals, and common ways of acting.

If children's expertise in literacy is to be made apparent in this kind of way, a wide range of activities is needed to provide opportunities for it to happen. Many types of reading and writing activities and language events have to take place if a teacher is to learn about a child's various forms of expertise, not only in topics and experience but also in their patterns of discourse and of teaching and learning.

The job of the teacher, then, is to use activities at school to look for a particular child's knowledge of, and ways of, using written language. This should not be limited to conventional knowledge and skills; for example, types of alphabet knowledge or pencil-handling skills. The teacher can search for and utilise evidence of a child's experience of literacy activities in his or her family. The teacher in the above interview also specifically mentioned looking to make use of older or more expert children in the classroom, enabling the new children to employ their expertise in observational learning acquired in peer and sibling groups.

The management issues raised cannot be fully addressed here. This is partly because our focus is not on classroom management, and partly, and more importantly, because the literature describes a variety of management styles used by teachers who are effective with children of diversity. For example, Ladson-Billings identified two teachers of African American children who differed in some respects in how structured their teaching was. But Ladson-Billings (1992) and others draw some commonalities about effective management styles (Au, 1993; Dyson, 1999a). One is that teachers establish the classroom as a community of learners in which peer-to-peer and teacher-to-student relationships are respectful, where roles are clearly defined, and where all community members have a high degree of responsibility.

In a well-organised community of learners, activities occur that enable children's cultural identities to be seen and heard. This need was recognised by some teachers in the Native Schools in New Zealand. An in-service talk on "oral expression" given to teachers of these schools in 1939 emphasised the value of sharing time to enable the teacher to bring the child's knowledge into the classroom:

She must discover that background; she must find out wherein lie the child's interests. She has him for some four or five hours a day. What of the other nineteen hours? ... She must realise that she can only build her contribution to his education on what has gone before. Then how to establish this tone in the room of genuine interest in the child as an individual? It will be found in the periods of free conversation, when the child's expression is stimulated through the sympathetic tone of the room and through the widening of his horizon by fresh experiences. (McNaughton, 2001, page 125)

Common experiences as a basis

The reference in the quotation to "fresh experiences" leads us to a second route, which is to create common experiences. When teachers deliberately create such experiences with children, the experiences themselves become the source of common topics and shared purposes, thereby reducing some of the work of discovering these things. In this way, the teacher can know what to incorporate, at least at the level of experiences and topics. However, the teaching still needs to be managed – the level of incorporation depends on whether or not children and teachers can easily share perspectives, and this depends on the structuring of the shared event.

Building shared experiences into the curriculum was a strategy employed by some of the teachers in New Zealand's Native Schools. The schools were situated in rural communities, and the experiences might involve a trip to the city or the use of plants from the local bush in nature studies. These experiences created a basis for curriculum subjects such as art and music as well as science, and reading and writing activities could be developed within and from them. In New Zealand, these all came to be part of what was known as "language experience" in the curriculum.

The family and community as informants

Family members, including parents and older siblings at school, are a third route to acquiring information about children. This is especially so if their familiar knowledge is appreciated by teachers and if ways of communicating effectively between family members and teachers can be established. This route and the first overlap, as children's autobiographies and family histories can both be used as starting points.[7]

Teachers can use formal ways of finding out information from family members. The writing portfolios prepared by parents that we described earlier in this chapter are one such example. However, as we noted then, what a teacher sees in such an exercise is closely tied to their ideas about literacy generally. The danger is that family voices can be difficult to hear and children's constructions difficult to see when teachers' ideas remain focused on conventional academic signposts.

The ubiquitous parent–teacher meetings offer a platform for sharing information about literacy learning across settings in linguistically and culturally diverse communities. Various writers describe how these conferences can provide useful information, but, as we noted with the devising of shared experiences, the care taken in structuring any meeting determines how effective it is, as do the histories of contact between parents and teachers before and after it.[8]

Meetings between families and teachers involve a meeting of minds similar to the one between teachers and children. Again, there is the question of how each participant comes to know about what the other knows, values, and acts on and what the goals of the joint activity are. The potential for misunderstanding is always present – hence there is a need for teachers and families to develop a shared approach to the task.[9]

Being an expert in making connections

Teachers' effectiveness in making connections with learners depends on various facets of their expertise, including:

- how they see the nature of teaching, learning, language, and literacy;
- the degree to which they are aware of, and how they promote, the resources of families and communities;
- how they structure events within and outside the classroom to gain better knowledge of children's expertise.

A final word on what this expertise should enable us to do comes from one of the teachers studied by Ladson-Billings:

I find that much of what we claim we want to teach kids they already know in some form. I want to know what they know so that we can make some natural and relevant connections to their lives. Sometimes my black children will have information about home remedies or stories and folktales they've heard from their grandparents. We take those stories and remedies and write them up, compare notes, see how their knowledge compares with so-called traditional knowledge .... My students know about things like community politics and police brutality. I can't feed them a steady diet of cute little animal stories and happy middle-class kids. Their experiences have to be part of our curriculum, too. (Ladson-Billings, 1994, pages 52–53)

End Notes

1 Various writers have examined the nature of learning in communities of practice, using the idea that learning can be seen as a form of apprenticeship, both for children and adults – a process of initially peripheral and increasingly central participation in the practices of that community (Lave and Wenger, 1991; Rogoff, 1990).

2 Folk pedagogies operate from the beliefs, often intuitive and deeply ingrained, that teachers hold and the assumptions that they make about how children learn. Olson and Bruner (1996) describe the theories (often intuitive) that we hold about helping children to learn and, more generally, about how their minds and our minds work. The latter theories are more generally termed "folk psychologies". All these theories are present in teaching decisions and reflect deeply ingrained cultural beliefs as well as developing professional ideas.

3 These description are reported in McNaughton (2001) and come from a larger study of the transition to school (Phillips, McNaughton, and MacDonald, 2001).

4 Summaries of the relationships between knowledge of students and instruction can be found in Darling-Hammond (1997). The analysis of the IEA data was reported by Wilkinson (1998).

5 Au (1993) and Delpit (1995) have described teachers' corrections of Black English. Continued correction such as this has predictable effects. It reduces accuracy and self-regulation in oral reading, thereby limiting children's learning within and across reading texts (McNaughton, 1987). This, of course, does not include the effect on a child of getting an explicit message about the inadequacy of their language (and hence identity).

6 These concepts of how curriculum spaces are created, and how teachers create lesson structures to enable voices to be heard, are elaborated in Dyson (1999a; 1999b; 2001).

7 There are many examples in the studies of effective teachers and programmes of using family autobiographies and histories (Delpit, 1995; Ladson-Billings, 1992; Paratore, 1995; Trumbull, Rothstein-Fiskh, and Greenfield, 2001). More broadly, the use of family experiences in classroom literacy activities provides further ways of sharing information about children (Moll, 1999).

8 Paratore, Hindin, Krol-Sinclair, Duran, Emig, and McClure (2000) provide evidence of home literacy portfolios serving as a basis for focused and rich discussion about home literacy activities in teacher–parent conferences. Darling-Hammond (1997) also describes aspects of effective parent conferences, and there are examples in Ladson-Billings's (1992) studies of finding out from parents about the knowledge that children

bring with them to the classroom, including learning from parents about the ways in which they have educated their children.

9   The processes of developing shared understanding between teachers and families are discussed in McNaughton (1995).

Part Three

PART 3

Unlocking the Unfamiliar

Part 3

Unlocking the Unfamiliar

Imagine joining an exclusive and secret society for which you do not yet know the rules. Or imagine that you have gone to live in a very different country from your own, and the rules and expectations of its culture are quite unfamiliar. The immediate question is – how do you get to learn the rules? Underlying that question is – where are the rules? Are they written down? Could someone act as a guide? Then other questions may come; for example, why do things this way?

This may be the order of the task facing some children going to school. One can conceive of classrooms as cultures in microcosm, with their own idiosyncratic tasks, patterns of behaving, and rules of engagement. This means that children, especially those not from mainstream communities or the communities that their teachers represent, are engaged in cross-cultural communication with their teachers. Viewing classrooms as cultural settings has the following kind of significance for the meeting of minds:

> If you are not already a participant in the culture of power, being told explicitly the rules of that culture makes acquiring power easier .... [M]embers of any culture transmit information implicitly to co-members. However, when implicit codes are attempted across cultures, communication frequently breaks down. Each cultural group is left saying, **"Why don't those people say what they mean?"** as well as, **"What's wrong with them, why don't they understand?"** [author's emphasis]. (Delpit, 1995, page 25)

From this perspective, the meeting of minds is to do not only with building on the familiar, as we argued in the previous chapters, but also with unlocking the unfamiliar. The confusion around what is required in classrooms and what understanding is needed to unlock the rules for what happens in them is addressed in this part. We argue that a process of coming to be aware is needed – a companion to, and complement of, the process of incorporation that we have discussed in the previous four chapters. It is the process of discriminating the rules and requirements for expertise.

In Chapter 6, *Creating a Shared Understanding*, we explore again the classroom conditions – the qualities of the curriculum and its associated activities – that promote the development of an awareness that can help teachers to teach and children to learn literacy effectively.

In Chapter 7, *Strategies for Developing Shared Awareness*, we identify the strategies for creating shared awareness that are promoted by the classroom conditions, and we examine the evidence for their effectiveness.

In Chapter 8, *Awareness and Reading Comprehension*, we look at how strategies for developing awareness can apply in the development of expertise in comprehension at the beginnings of literacy instruction in school.

In Chapter 9, *More on Being an Expert*, we extend our exploration of the need for teachers to develop expert levels of awareness, both of themselves and their children, if the rules and patterns of expertise required in the classroom are to be unlocked for children.

Chapter 6

Creating a Shared Understanding

Overview of the chapter

Community, curriculum, and language

What elements of the curriculum create conditions specifically related to the task of unlocking the unfamiliar in effective teaching and learning? We explore three in this chapter, extending those elements that we explored in Chapter 2. One is the need to create a community of practising learners. Another is a curriculum of variation. The third is a curriculum that enables awareness to develop. There are several reasons for introducing these additional elements. They all have to do with creating greater clarity and shared understanding about classroom tasks. But featuring prominently in each of the elements is the role of classroom language – and we turn first to examine the nature of classroom language and what that implies for children's learning.

The nature of classroom learning

For teachers and learners to engage effectively in unlocking the unfamiliar, the curriculum needs to enable them to develop a shared understanding of what classroom literacy instruction actually requires. This principle underlies the co-construction model of teaching and learning that we have been elaborating in this book. This holds that the more teachers and learners come to share understanding about goals, performance of tasks, participation, and the meaning of guidance in the classroom, the more effective the interactions between them will be.

The novice and classroom language

For the child as learner and novice participant, various questions arise as they engage in classroom activities. What are these activities for, how do you do them, what do you need to know? The answers can come from the social context – the meanings of classroom activities are conveyed and defined by what happens when the child does things with teachers and peers or on their own. But often, initially, at least, the meanings are conveyed by the language that the teacher uses.

The language that children need

So, in literacy, unlocking what is unfamiliar becomes partly a question of the language that children need to acquire to be successful. Language is an object of study as they come to learn how to match their oral language to a set of symbols and to manipulate their language using those symbols. In this sense, "coming to know the language" means developing that knowledge of language as an object, understandings described in such concepts as the alphabetic principle and phonemic awareness.

But becoming expert in the language of the classroom also includes the language used as the medium for instruction because much of what is taught takes place verbally, as teachers question, direct, prompt, comment, and evaluate. Getting to know what the teacher means is a task at two levels for the child. At one level, it involves a child coming to understand the actual vocabulary and sentence structures that teachers use. It also means coming to understand *how* those words and sentences are used – in classroom discourse generally and literacy activities in particular.

Even the simplest utterance from the teacher requires some figuring out by a new learner. So when a teacher says, for example, "What word does that one look like?" or "I wonder what will happen next?" or "Would that make sense?", a new learner has to know what is expected of them. The child has to figure out whether rhetorical questions should be answered directly, for example, or which elements in a comparison are the ones that the teacher assumes are important. So children need to learn how to use the language of the classroom, and that this may involve quite different uses and meanings from those of their language at home.

Classroom language and contextualisation

Educators and researchers have commonly argued that the core difference between the language used outside the classroom and the language required in school activities is one of contextualisation. Outside the classroom, they argue, language is contextualised. That is, speakers rely on there being a basis of shared experiences upon which to draw, and communication in face-to-face interactions is derived from shared understandings about events, meanings, and uses (Gee, 1998). Inside the classroom, by comparison, the argument continues, language is decontextualised. It needs to be explicit, to express literal meanings, and to make logical connections and can not rely on familiarity between speakers to convey meaning.

In literacy instruction, an analysis of patterns of discourse and the requirements of literacy in the classroom reveals a general emphasis on precision, explicitness, and clarity.[1] This includes an ability to create oral texts whose logic and structure are made clear to audiences and to engage with texts in what Chang-Wells and Wells (1993) call an epistemic mode – that is, to be able to check, extend, and revise an oral or written text and the learner's understanding of it.

Different types of context

To say simply, however, that decontextualised language is used in school and contextualised language is used in homes is problematic for two reasons. One is the presence of different languages at school – uses and styles differ across lessons and subjects, and the distinctions made are not hard and fast. But the major difference between language inside and language outside school lies not so much in whether one is contextualised and the other is decontextualised. It lies more in *types* of contextualisation. James Gee replaces the term "decontextualised" with "linguistically contextualised", as he explains:

School-based, academic, specialist, and public-sphere forms of language are "linguistically contextualised" in the important sense that, in all cases, the child is learning a new (variety of) language, a language different from the language of the "lifeworld". They are "linguistically contextualised" as well, in the important sense that many of the experiences children must have to be able to contextualise this new variety of language are experiences with new types of texts and talk. In this sense, ideas about language acquisition and development are crucial to all school learning. But to understand a new specialist variety of language, children must learn to actively contextualise it in terms of the new experiences they are having in and out of school, not only with new types of text and talk but also with new ways of thinking, believing, knowing, feeling, acting, and interacting with other people and various sorts of places, objects, tools, and technologies. ... [These] forms of language often require us to exit our lifeworlds and construe contexts based on experiences we have outside these lifeworlds ... from the outset, [advantaged children's] induction into specialist domains has incorporated from early on, some of the practices and values of specialist domains, though, of course, in attenuated forms (for example, early reading of "children's literature", a bridge to the specialist domain of "literature" proper). For many minority and poor children, by contrast, no such bridges exist or are built. We rarely build on their experiences and on their very real, distinctive lifeworld knowledge. In fact, these children are often asked, in the process of being exposed to specialist domains, to deny the value of their lifeworlds and their communities in reference to those of more advantaged children. (Gee, 1998, pages xiii–xiv)

Experiencing the rules for language contexts

What is implied here is that teachers need to have a set of strategies for making the rules of "linguistically contextualised" language more accessible to those students who, because of their backgrounds, have had little experience of those rules. The strategies would enable students to be both explicitly taught the new ways of using language and informally socialised into them. Teachers would need to be conscious of their role as cultural mentors who enable children to become functioning members of the classroom community.

These two processes, informal socialisation and explicit teaching, are essentially the two endpoints of a teaching and learning continuum. At one end, there is immersion in everyday practices with an apprenticeship style of becoming expert. At the other end, there is explicit description and direct learning of what is required. In the next chapter, we will identify strategies that lie along this continuum. Here we need to outline the conditions of the curriculum that would enable these strategies to occur.

A curriculum for a community of learners

Given this analysis of language contexts, some additional features have to be identified in the wide curriculum that we outlined in Chapter 2. What does the presence of an immersion-explicit teaching continuum require of a wide curriculum, especially for those children who might find activities most unfamiliar? Such children need a curriculum that enables them quickly to become familiar with the core ways of using oral and written language in the classroom – to own these classroom ways, to want to use them, and to enjoy using them (Cazden, 1993). The best set of conditions for this can be described as a community of practice or, in the context of a classroom, a community of practising learners. To elaborate this concept, we need to develop the discussion of our model of teaching and learning a little further.

The model of teaching and learning revisited

Classroom activities allow for various patterns of teaching and learning that, in turn, can create different learning conditions in classrooms. These patterns may be as seemingly disparate as a teacher's direct teaching of, say, a letter–sound relationship or a child's personal discovery of the same relationship. Their forms and outcomes, however, can all be understood within the general model introduced in Chapter 2 – that is, that learning and development are co-constructed by teacher and learner through structured activities. Participants' goals and ways of participating are transformed over time as younger or less expert members come to be more expert.[2]

The model as a descriptive framework

This is not an idealised model of how teaching and learning should occur. Rather, it is a descriptive framework for understanding the various components. These include the central role of personal as well as joint activities, the various patterns of interacting within activities, and the relationships that these patterns of interaction have with different forms of learning. For example, didactic teaching (say, telling a child a letter–sound association) is associated with particular ways of participating, and doing this in the presence of particular goals and patterns of learning. Indirectly helping a child to express themselves in a piece of writing is associated with other ways of participating.

Judging effectiveness in teaching and learning

This model also provides ways of asking questions about the effectiveness of teaching and learning. Judging effectiveness here becomes a matter of looking at the outcomes associated with particular configurations of activities. Given their purposes – for example, to develop ways of comprehending meanings in texts – are the configurations suitable? Do they enable learning that meets these purposes to occur?

The development of "learning identities"

The model also assumes that there are complex relationships between a child's development and activities in the classroom. This is because the child is constructing ideas about literacy from a variety of activities within and outside classrooms. Moreover, there are multiple activities provided for the child to do this. To add to the complexity, activities can be well or poorly co-ordinated within and across settings. This complexity helps to explain something that took researchers some time to understand – that children can learn to read and write under different curricula.[3]

Children's learning and development occur as they participate in the activities of their community. In the process, they come to understand the roles and responsibilities required in these activities. Similarly, in classrooms, the enacted curriculum provides channels for promoting certain forms of expertise through patterns of teaching and learning in activities. In this curriculum, adults collaborate with the children and provide them with guidance and modelling. Group relations develop among class members as they learn to take responsibility both for their own contributions to learning in the classroom and for the group's learning.

All this means that the curriculum and the various ways of teaching and learning influence what children learn to become, as working members of a community. In the culture of the classroom, children's identities as learners are taking form. For example, if the need is to have children learn in ways that lead to extensive personal practice of, control over, and innovation with adult-like forms of reading and writing, then the ideal classroom in which this can happen is one that promotes a community of those particular sorts of learners.

A community of learners in practice

Organisations as diverse as sports clubs, Alcoholics Anonymous, or Girl Guides form communities of practice. A community of learners is similar – with shared practices around the core job of learning.[4] In its ideal form, a community of practice has a history of its members learning together in a style characterised by mutual engagement in a joint enterprise using a shared repertoire of activities.

Effective communities have activities that define their core social practice – their reason for being. In order to become fully functioning members of such a community, novices have to engage in the core practice, and the more expert members of the group need to create the environment in which this can happen. The activities are "meaningful" because engaging in them is why one belongs to the group. They are "authentic" in that they define what it means to be an expert in that community. If the activities are not meaningful or authentic, the community is a sham or exists for reasons other than the ones novices think that they join for.

Meaningfulness and authenticity in literacy instruction

"Meaningful" and "authentic" are words often used when referring to literacy instruction but not often defined. Defining them in this context will help us to understand the ways in which a curriculum can enhance awareness among learners and teachers of the rules of engagement. Activities that are authentic and meaningful are those that make sense to children as having adult-like purposes. Children come to see, hear, be moved by, and practise some "real life" ways of reading and writing. If, for example, the activities are to do with reading to comprehend, to evaluate, and to appreciate, then the meaningful and authentic ways in which experts perform such tasks should be present, at least in nascent forms, in the classroom, too.[5]

How does this apply in the classroom? There are some obvious examples from the curricula for science and mathematics. Children should be taught to do science – if you like, act as scientists – and not just acquire scientific facts, or to be mathematicians and not just learn a set of mathematical skills (Bransford, Brown, and Cocking, 1999; Wood, 1998). In literacy, children need to be immersed in the very activities that are fundamental to the social practices valued by the curriculum – which are, generally speaking, the activities that define the sorts of writers and readers valued by the school.[6]

In the case of writing, here are some examples of authentic and meaningful uses of writing in the community:

- writing to establish and keep networks in place (for example, when letters and emails are swapped between family members);
- writing to convince others (for example, in presenting a case to the tax department or preparing a full curriculum vitae for a job interview);
- writing to capture and narrate experience when we construct or repeat a family history.

There are parallels and additional practices associated with the workplace – summarising documents, sending memos, critically analysing political messages and advertising, and evaluating narratives. If these are all valued practices for a curriculum, then some apprenticeship in using these forms is needed in classrooms.

Participation in the group

We have argued that classrooms are, in some respects, cultural settings. The formation of a learner's identity – the process of becoming a working member of the group – is part of becoming enculturated.[7] A curriculum that contributes to children unlocking the unfamiliar is one that enables group participation and co-operation to develop. This sort of community of learners can be created through specific activities in a curriculum. The work of Brown, Campione, Palincsar, and their colleagues (Brown, 1994; Brown and Campione, 1994; Palincsar, Brown and Campione, 1993) has demonstrated one facet of group practices in urban classrooms serving communities of cultural diversity. One of the basic principles is a sense of group participation:

> *What if classrooms were designed explicitly to capitalize on varieties of talent to provide multiple "ways in" – through art, drama, technological skills, content knowledge, reading, writing, teaching, social facilitation and so forth? Indeed, it is very much our intention to increase diversity ... [and] nonconformity in the distribution of expertise and interests, so everyone can benefit from the subsequent richness of available knowledge. The essence of teamwork is pooling expertise.*
> (Brown, 1994, page 10)

The ideal classrooms that they have created feature individual responsibility coupled with communal sharing. Teachers expect and teach for diversity of expertise within the classroom. This spread of expertise does not occur by chance – it is deliberately engineered through specific instructional strategies.[8] It also occurs incidentally as children "major" in particular facets of a research topic. What this means in reading, for example, is that while everyone needs, and gets, to learn the basics of decoding and comprehension, the diversifying of interests increases the knowledge and skills available to the group as a whole. The ways of carrying out activities are very familiar – so the forms of co-operative research or comprehension are well known, and this, in itself, enhances the sense of community.

Shared discourse

As we noted at the outset of this chapter, language use is central to a sense of community, and this is evidenced in the classrooms in which Brown has worked. Constructive discussion, questioning, and criticism are both familiar and expected. Multiple zones of development are available to the children and provide a variety of sites for their learning, both with adults and peers. Shared talk is central to the operation of the community, so that the community can build on its expertise through members finding out and taking ideas and vocabulary from each other, as well as adding to them.

Evidence for effectiveness

Brown's programme of research demonstrates how a classroom with these features affects the learning of literacy, and we will include descriptions of this in the next three chapters. In Brown's work, the evidence of effectiveness is compelling, particularly in children's acquisition of scientific knowledge and in their comprehension. In the community created in these classrooms, activities specifically focus on these areas. But learning outcomes are not limited to these, because there is evidence for transfer of processes, such as reasoning by analogy to topics yet to be a focus.

There is also evidence that this sort of community of learning can produce more effective learning in other areas; for example, in paying greater attention to conceptual understanding (and sometimes less to mechanics). And the children are more likely to work collaboratively outside the classroom and build on each other's ideas as a consequence of their membership of the community (Rogoff, Matusov, and White, 1996).

These studies offer an important insight about communities of learning. Attempts to produce such a community need to do more than create compartmentalised changes. It is not sufficient just to add a co-operative learning session or some group projects that require co-operation into the classroom curriculum. Indeed, that can create confusion.[9]

A curriculum for familiar practice and variation

The argument to this point is that the need for unlocking what is unfamiliar is met by a curriculum that creates a community of learners. On what should that community act? For such a community, the curriculum needs to provide the extensive use and production of texts, with planned variation in the sorts of texts used and produced.

The need for extensive experience

Expert performance and learning that is durable and can transfer across situations come from a deep understanding of a domain of learning. Experts know about the variety of contexts in which their skills can operate, and they can spot new examples of contexts. They understand underlying principles, such as how the requirements of tasks are similar and different one from another. In classroom literacy, this kind of deep understanding depends on the children having extensive and repeated experience across contexts and across types of tasks, with both success and failure at them (Bransford, Brown, and Cocking, 1999).

Balancing the new and the familiar

A hallmark of effective beginning literacy instruction is the careful selection of texts for reading. This ensures that the texts chosen do not outstrip the learner's background knowledge and current language skills, that they contribute to what is called the learner's "zone of proximal development".[10] Maintaining this balance between the familiar and the new applies to all levels of texts – from individual letters and sounds through to general forms of narrative and expository texts.

From the beginning, the curriculum needs to promote, through a rich variety of reading texts and types of writing, controlled practice with familiar texts and controlled exposure to what is unfamiliar. In reading texts, the variation comes from differing types of narratives or expositions, ways of presentation, and topics. In writing, children can develop a similar variety of texts, and, when teachers create space, hybrid forms too.

Practice and variation: the case of beginning reading texts

We can illustrate the significance of carefully balancing familiar and unfamiliar texts by looking at how children acquire vocabulary from reading. The extent of a child's vocabulary is an important determiner of reading comprehension. A normal rate of vocabulary growth in the early grades is about six new words per school day, at least half of this happening independently of any deliberate effort by schools.[11] Textbooks, and what teachers do with them, can be a major source of access to new vocabulary (see Chapter 8). But classrooms, as environments for learning, do not provide optimal conditions for picking up new vocabulary.

Casting the net of written words wide

One reason for limited effectiveness lies in restricting instruction to the use of basal texts. The evidence suggests that the narrow range of vocabulary and limited rate of introducing new words in basal series restrict vocabulary growth. But there is a dilemma here. Richly worded books by children's authors ("trade" books) can be very difficult, especially for children from diverse urban communities, because of the unknown words and unfamiliar language structures that these books might contain.

We have outlined some solutions to this in the strategies described in Chapter 3, such as priming children's background knowledge or incorporating features of their language and knowledge within their reading texts to increase familiarity. In Chapter 7, we will outline other strategies to increase children's awareness of the features of text and thus to expand their control over school language. But each of these sets of strategies depends on a curriculum in which there actually are books that have a wide and increasing range of words. It is difficult to expand vocabulary if only basals are used. It is possible to present rich texts to make them fit the children, and it is possible to write books for children that will afford them a rich haul from their lexical net.

A curriculum with a focus on developing awareness

If a curriculum is to provide conditions for strategies that can increase children's immersion and develop their awareness, it needs to enable a community of learners with extensive and varied practice to be created. But this is not enough either. It is also necessary to ensure that carefully planned explication accompanies this kind of apprenticeship.

Rogoff, Matusov, and White (1996) describe the difficulties that adults who are novices experience when they come into an adult community of learners. The community in their example was a co-operative school run by teachers and parents. Difficulties were greatest when ideas about the nature of teaching and learning held by newly arrived teachers and parents were different from those held by existing members of the community.

This community used an apprenticeship system that emphasised learning through observing, discussing, and participating rather than by being handed information – that is, through direct instruction of rules. There were various reasons for this, including the need for new generations of teachers and parents to be part of the process of decision making and developing new ideas. The principles of learning in the community were not considered to be a fixed recipe for action, and creative innovations were deemed necessary. Nevertheless, new teachers and new parents consistently called for more explicit directives. The reason for this, apart from wanting to short-circuit difficulties, is that adults have available to them well-practised strategies for making unfamiliar social situations familiar – not being able to untangle confusions with simple rules can be uncomfortable.

If this (very durable, as it turns out) learning community created confusion and difficulty for its adult newcomers, how much more might unfamiliar territories such as classrooms do so for newly arrived children?[12] The solution is to make sure that carefully planned explication accompanies apprenticeship.

Promoting awareness through explanation

At what point might it be possible to teach children explicitly about how classroom activities work? What do we know about the development of awareness in children that might enable us to answer such a question?

The development of awareness

Awareness in the sense of thinking about one's thinking is made up of analysis and control. With language, this entails being able to reflect on language and its uses as well as being able to monitor and plan language uses intentionally, in both production and comprehension.[13]

Young children learn how to use language in many ways, most of which are not under conscious control. That is how they are able to talk effectively as young members of their communities. This knowledge of language use starts early in life and is well developed by entry to school.[14] But conscious analysis and control develop more slowly. At school, the awareness comes about largely due to school literacy requirements and tuition.

The act of writing, for example, compels some analysis and control because, for the writer, language becomes an observable object, and he or she needs to solve problems that are not easily solved automatically. Likewise, learners can get access to their knowledge about writing and reading from interactions with teachers and peers that make it obvious what the learners know and can do. In this way, the role of teachers and peers is to enhance the learner's internalisation of awareness. If awareness comes from being able to act, then acting in emergent forms of reading and writing is a platform for analysing the features of one's performance and developing ways of controlling that performance.

The growth of awareness can be plotted in all dimensions of written language – phonological, syntactic, semantic, pragmatic, and textual. Each dimension is affected by this development and, at least initially, is independent of the others.

Phonemic and phonological awareness

With the development of phonemic and phonological awareness, for example, there appears to be a progression that builds from implicit knowledge of chunks of sound, such as syllables, and a growing awareness of more specific units, such as onsets and rimes. From this emerging awareness, children develop a fine-grained sensitivity to, and control over, individual phonemes – the smallest segments of sound that make a difference to the meaning of a word, such as the difference between 'hat' and 'hit'. This phonemic awareness develops as children receive formal instruction. But the awareness that words involve sequences of phonemes develops gradually and can be present much earlier. For example, preschoolers can often hear individual phonemes at the beginning of words composed of single-phoneme onsets (common in English in examples such as /d/ in dog and /c/ in cat).

The presence of developmental sequences has significance for planning teaching acts with activities (see Chapter 4). For example, monitoring children's implicit ("epilinguistic") knowledge provides a basis on which to plan, as does knowing about their developing awareness at a syllabic level.

Awareness of overall patterns in text

Perhaps more important to any discussion about curriculum conditions is the finding that awareness also develops at more complex text levels.[16] Children gradually develop "frameworks of construal" or cognitive models for discourse and text patterns. The significance of these frameworks is shown in studies that manipulate what type of text the reader believes a passage comes from (for example, autobiography or fiction). How a text is interpreted is, in part, determined by this framework. Interpretive patterns are part of readers' cognitive skills, enabling them to know more about a text than they have been told.

Emergent awareness

Young children develop early versions of these forms of awareness. There are descriptions of classrooms that show that children in year 1 can be aware of the difference between fiction and non-fiction, and there is at least one demonstration that children can be taught such distinctions in the first year.[17] But, in the early years of schooling, children rarely know what genre they are working in until, by trial and error, they get it right.

Building an emergent awareness

The implications of these findings is that it is possible for teachers to build on each of these levels of emergent awareness, including that of understanding types of texts.[18] But there is an issue here to do with how explicit instruction could or should be. Feldman and Kalmar (1996) see no reason to fear that the explicit teaching of young children about text genres would divert effort away from learning basic elements. On the contrary, they see this as potentially helping to make tasks less ambiguous. Making the frameworks more explicit would help children to see elements such as sounds and letters in many different contexts. Therefore, confusions about which elements are essential might be resolved more easily.

But there are provisos to this call.[19] The problem with direct teaching is that texts are complex and, as with grammar, the task of specifying all the rules is daunting. The simplification needed, and the consequent overcategorisation, might limit the opportunities for incidental learning described in Chapter 2. Also, in the absence of a degree of implicit knowledge – knowledge that children already have but are not yet aware of – explicit teaching may confuse by drawing the child's attention away from getting that knowledge in place. Moreover, when they write, children invent and play with hybrid kinds of texts not easily categorised. Teaching of or to rules would stultify this play and innovation.

On the other hand, large amounts of direct instruction may not be needed. Freedman (1993) showed that by grade five children had developed an understanding of typical story structures anyway, seemingly without formal instruction. This debate parallels the arguments about the explicit and direct teaching of phonological knowledge and phonemic awareness, and the same confusions about those matters that we came across in Chapter 4 can be found here.[20]

Developing awareness of how to participate

This chapter has used the model of teaching and learning to identify the conditions that a curriculum should provide in order for awareness to develop. That model sees teaching and learning as a matter of joint participation from which, through shared understanding and co-construction, expertise emerges. From this perspective, the need to be aware is best represented as a need to know (in the sense of analyse and control) how to participate. Again, from this perspective, labels for items and concepts ("this is a syllable", "this is fiction") may help children to discriminate what to act on as they participate. But having a shared understanding in a community is a critical part of instruction that includes such labelling of things and the development of awareness about what to do.

The implications of this model of teaching and learning for the conditions of the curriculum are contained in Gee's (1998) "bill of rights" for children for whom schools are risky places. He claims that children have a right to:

- extensive participation in authentic and meaningful social practices involving talk, texts, tools, and technologies and that these practices should not denigrate their own experiences from outside school;
- overt instruction that provides them with guidance in, and scaffolding for, classroom practices;
- awareness of the make-up of classroom tasks and how their own knowledge fits with what is expected in the performance of these tasks;

- development of expertise in classroom activities that they can transform in ways that offer them the power to innovate for their own social, cultural, and political purposes.

In Chapter 7, we explore strategies for achieving the first two of these rights in beginning literacy instruction.

End Notes

1 Descriptions of typical differences between home and school uses of language have been described by a number of researchers (Cazden, 1988; Hemphill and Snow, 1998; Wood, 1998). Chang-Wells and Wells (1993) also argue that the core functions that literacy in school serves include building and disciplining information in a systematic and formal manner, fixing on meaning as a permanent product out of the context of the original writing or reading and in ways that allow for comparisons, interpretations, and revision, ultimately leading to being aware of the processes and outcomes of thinking.

2 Some discussion of different approaches within the general ideas of sociocultural theorising is contained in Forman, Minick, and Stone (1993) and Olson and Torrance (1996). In addition, there is specific discussion of the variation in patterns of teaching and learning in McNaughton (1995) and Rogoff, Matusov, and White (1996).

3 Clearly, children learn to read under different programmes of reading instruction (McNaughton, 1995).

4 Detailed analyses of communities of practice are contained in Wenger (1998), and of communities of learners in Rogoff, Matusov and White (1996).

5 This is a fundamental sort of practice, one that is situated in the very activities that define what the community is for. There is a venerable history of arguing for situated practice in education from educational philosophers such as James Dewey through to contemporary psychologists such as Bruner and Cole. What this sense of situated practice means for classroom literacy is that there is a match between how reading and writing is being learned and what it means to be a reader and writer (Wenger, 1998).

6 The definition of real world activities is not straightforward for at least two reasons. One is that different sorts of social practices exist; another is that practices change over time. This means that a curriculum may or may not recognise contemporary forms and those forms that are not mainstream forms (Luke and Luke, 2001).

7 Wenger argues that identity formation is true for education in general. "Education in its deepest sense and at whatever age it takes place, concerns the opening of identities – exploring new ways of being that lie beyond our current state ... it places students on an outbound trajectory toward a broad field of possible identities. Education is not merely formative – it is transformative." (Wenger, 1998, page 263)

8 Two such strategies have received intense research scrutiny. These are "Reciprocal Teaching" and "jigsaw of co-operative learning", where research groups working on subtopics need to pool their expertise to complete the full topic.

9 Further striking support for the concept of community comes from descriptions of teachers shown to be effective with linguistically and culturally diverse children (Delpit,

1995; Ladson-Billings, 1994; and Heath, 1983). In these classrooms, irrespective of the particular programmes of reading or writing that have been adopted, there is a community at work. There is a clear sense among the children of being a functioning member contributing to a culture of learning.

10 Further descriptions of this concept from Vygotsky (1978) can be found in Wood (1998), Tharp and Gallimore (1988), and McNaughton (1995).

11 This estimation comes from Biemiller (1999).

12 Details of the role of direct instruction and immersion for adult participants is provided in Rogoff, Turkanis, and Bartlett (2001).

13 Further descriptions of awareness and of general and specific models for cognition and language can be found in Camps and Milian (2000), Clay (1999), Karmiloff-Smith (1992), and Gombert (1992).

14 Although language development is not by any means completed by this time (Pinker, 1999; Wood, 1998).

15 See Goswami (2001). Such sequences reflect the nature of becoming aware of English. Children learning a non-alphabetic language may not develop such fine distinctions at sub-word levels.

16 The descriptions come from Feldman and Kalmar (1996), and specific demonstrations of this knowledge can be found in Duthie (1994) and Smith and Elley (1997).

17 See Feldman and Kalmar (1996), Duthie (1994) and Smith and Elley (1997) op. cit.

18 Hemphill and Snow (1996) claim that the middle-class child coming to school has the advantage of exposure to a variety and wide array of genres. This is a further version of the continuity hypothesis, which argues that exposing children to a wide variety of types means that they are better able to spot features of classroom genres.

19 These qualifications have been voiced by Smith and Elley (1997) and Dyson (1999).

20 Freedman's own solution to the debate is to argue that explicit teaching might be beneficial when children are involved in authentic tasks and authentic contexts involving the targeted genre; that is, teaching to this knowledge only in the context of acting with this knowledge, as in Type 1 teaching acts for phonological knowledge (see Chapter 4).

Chapter 7

Strategies for Developing Shared Awareness

Overview of the chapter

The comprehensible classroom

This chapter returns to the subject of Chapter 3 – teaching strategies. The central question here is how to teach culturally and linguistically diverse children so that they can more easily unlock what is unfamiliar. An answer is contained in James Gee's bill of rights, outlined at the end of Chapter 6, for those children for whom school is a risky business.

The first two of Gee's rights inform two approaches to the development of children's awareness of the forms and functions of language and literacy in the classroom. Both approaches are needed, and each is incomplete and relatively ineffective without the other. One approach concerns children's need for extensive experience of those literacy and language activities that are central to schooling success. The approach requires practice that takes place, not in isolation but in a functioning community of learners. The reasons for this were outlined in the previous chapter.

The other approach concerns children's need for explicit teaching of the ways of participating in classroom activities, the goals for participation, and the forms of expertise required. This second approach seems as straightforward as the first. But our discussion of the teaching of phonics in Chapter 4 alerted us to the special requirements for teaching to be explicit, direct, *and* effective.

However, even after having worked through this, there are still difficulties to face. Can young children on entry to school be aware of complex language forms and explicit and controlled ways of using language, as suggested in the last chapter? Can the rules associated with classroom language be unravelled in ways that are both comprehensible and usable to those children who have not been socialised into how language is used at school?[1]

Here we explore the details of what teachers actually do – the strategies that they have used and that researchers have studied – to enable this awareness to develop, and the evidence for the effectiveness of the strategies. It is possible to use these strategies, given the curriculum conditions discussed in the previous chapter.

There are two sections in this chapter: one on the strategies of *planned exposure* and the other on the strategies of *priming awareness*. In both, we aim to illustrate the principles behind the strategies. We also aim to examine the evidence that it is possible to boost "novice" children's awareness of classroom tasks so that their progress in learning to read and write is enhanced.

Structured immersion: the strategies of planned exposure

One of the rights for children that James Gee proposes is what he describes as lots of "situated practice". This means lots of hands-on experience of authentic and meaningful reading and writing activities in the classroom. This is an apprenticeship style of learning, where the learner is deeply engaged in seeing, hearing, being moved by, and practising literacy activities that make sense as "real world" things to do or ways to be.

This requirement makes good psychological sense and can be supported by research evidence. Repeated practice situated in the very activities that one needs to practise in order to become expert also seems common sense. However, it is surprising how unappreciated such a seemingly obvious point can be. For example, the evidence from research into vocabulary acquisition (see Chapter 2) is extraordinary in what it says about practice.

Why practice works
Acquiring vocabulary

Contemporary models of how word meanings are learned have been able to incorporate the incidental learning effects that we explored in Chapter 2. Thomas Landauer, for example, proposes a model of a learner's knowledge of vocabulary as a kind of semantic space where meanings are connected. The associations and linkages between words and passages fill this space, in which each word and any passage in the learner's language has its own place. The space comes into being from experiencing text.

Landauer's model demonstrates how human cognitive abilities often depend on immense amounts of experience for their development. The learner observes how often words occur in various contexts (such as sentences or paragraphs) relative to how often they occur in different contexts, and fits all these relations together.

> *Of the roughly 400 000 words that a typical seventh grader could have encountered in print but nowhere else, she knows the meaning of 10 today that she did not know yesterday. Amazingly, she saw only 2 or 3 of these in the*

interim. Moreover, when psychologists have tried teaching word meanings explicitly, they have not come close to normal rates. Traditional theories of word learning, which are based on specific concrete experiences with individual words, cannot account for these facts. However, when a very large number of other words is known, the indirect effects assumed [in the model] offer an explanation: Correctly mapping a few new relations can help to define many more. (Landauer, 1998, page 163)

The model accounts for the effects of incidental learning by showing the sensitivity of networks and links within this semantic space that enables new words to be learned. Again, we see the ubiquitous Matthew effects at work positively – the more one knows, the more one can learn.[2]

There is plenty of support for educators' and researchers' arguments that children who enter school less familiar with school tasks need more of what the school has to offer.[3] As the explanations above indicate, this is critical in matters of language acquisition such as vocabulary size, but the requirement goes across all aspects of literacy activities in the classroom.

Developing expertise in comprehension

The development of comprehension is also dependent on practice. The amount of a child's exposure to print is related to all aspects of their comprehension, including word knowledge, general knowledge, linguistic sensitivity, and knowledge about how to represent mental states in writing (for example, "concedes", "asserts", "implies", "suggests"). Research shows that any practice is efficacious, regardless of one's overall level of skill, and that negative Matthew effects are reversible from exposure to print.[4]

The effects of practice can also be seen in how proficient readers connect and relate ideas from their current reading to previous reading experiences. Contemporary examples of expert readers at school point out the readers' facility to create inter-textual links (Hartman, 1995). Making connections between texts influences readers' ability to predict text and their proficiency in using cueing systems within texts (Martens, Flurkey, Meyer, and Udell, 1999). Extensive experience with texts feeds into extended comprehension. The more experiences one has, the more textual resources there are to call upon.

Extensive and modulated use of texts

In Chapter 3, we quoted teachers from New Zealand's former Native Schools describing their invention of reading books with topics and language appropriate for the use of Māori children, who very often lived in rural communities. One of those teachers, referring to her work in the 1940s, went on to say how she wrote her own text:

> [I]n those days you'd introduce one word per page and then all the other words had to be words that had already been introduced. You kept the new words down to a minimum. (McNaughton, 2001, page 108)

Matching texts to skills

Here is the essence of this strategy – the careful use of many texts that create a balance of familiar with unfamiliar through exposing the reader to a wide range of textual elements, including words, sentences, illustrations, structure, and presentation, and matching up each of these with the reader's present skills. This practice was picked up in research observations of teachers identified as top practitioners in the teaching of reading in New Zealand classrooms (Wilkinson and Townsend, 2000). The observations revealed choices of texts that:

> ... provided appropriate levels of challenge and support for students ... not just in terms of the familiarity of words but also in terms of the print size, length of the selection, language structures, predictability of the language, text structure, genre, match between illustrations and print, and the prior knowledge required to comprehend the text. (Wilkinson and Townsend, 2000, page 469)

Varying repetition

The above study features one teacher, working in an urban school serving Māori and Pacific Islands families, who illustrates how her decisionmaking used both incorporation strategies (culturally based peer tutoring) and the sense of a community of learners. Within this, she managed the children's exposure to specific words by a judicious selection of texts, creating repeated exposures in different settings:

> T: I found that one of the words that two of the Red-1 level children were having trouble with was said, and so we need to push said. And three children in the Emergent group, [Vana, Ian, and David], should probably be able to pick up said quite easily, because they picked up I am and a quickly and easily. So I'm actually going to cross-group [Vana, Ian, and David] with the Red-1s, and when

I do the Red-1s' instructional reading, those three will be in with them and I'll push said *with them. So although it's actually not a change in group, just for this one aspect they're going to their own [the Emergent's] instructional reading, where I'm still going to be pushing* I am, *and* a, *and I might bring in* the *as well. They'll still be doing that, but they'll also be working on* said, *because we can use structures like "'I am a dog,' said Charlie girl."*

I: *Yes, and those structures come in at Red-1.*

T: *Yes, they come in at Red-1, you see.*

I: *Right.*

T: *And if [Vana, Ian, and David] pick up* said *and they're using* said *with their own group, then there'll be a sort of peer tutoring between the two, and they'll say to the other kids "oh that word's* said." *Therefore, I'm saying it to them, and so are [Vana, Ian, and David], so they'll get the input two ways there.* (Wilkinson and Townsend, 2000, pages 466–467)

Here, the teacher is systematically choosing texts for repetition of words and phrases. But the texts that the children might read and write will vary in other dimensions. The strategy entails systematically varying book types (such as narrative and expository), themes, and topics.[5] The same strategy can be seen in the structuring or writing sessions described in earlier chapters that allow children to produce various types of texts, including hybrid forms. In many of these descriptions, there is a strong sense of teacher mediation – that the teachers are highlighting or specifically making connections between the features of texts for which those particular texts have been selected. As we shall show in the second section of this chapter, it is likely that the strategy is most effective with that mediation.

Book floods

Additional evidence for the significance of extensive practice comes from studies of classrooms that, prior to the study, had few books and little teaching based on the extensive use of books. Under appropriate conditions, when these classrooms were flooded with many new books, there were significant gains in various measures of the children's literacy and language. "Appropriate conditions" included the systematic training of teachers in how to use the books frequently and as a basis for instruction; for example, in ways of reading to children. Educationally significant effects from this strategy have been found across all ages and types of students, including those in early childhood settings and those who have English as a second language.[6]

Code-switching in print

The description of this kind of strategy thus far involves children's immersion in texts varying in type and in features such as topic, sentence structure, or word usage. Another version of this strategy, described in previous chapters as incorporation, is the deliberate switching between ways of using language in the communities outside school and the forms typically used in classrooms. In this respect, the strategy models code-switching in oral and written language. Descriptions of this version of the strategy show the teachers deliberately teaching the connections and differences between the conventional English used in classrooms and the variations in discourse and dialects outside the classroom.

In Chapter 3, for example, there is a description of a teacher who effectively incorporated children's knowledge of rap music and hip hop culture into her literacy instruction. She copied out the words of a song by M.C. Hammer and gave the text to her students. Class volunteers sang the text, but, after the performance, the teacher admitted that she didn't understand it and asked the children to help her. To do this, she modelled a translation exercise. She used an overhead transparency on which the lyrics were written with the children's and her shared interpretations written underneath them in more formal standard English. Her comments show that she saw the children as bilingual, and that she could teach these children to go from one form of language to the other.[7]

Modelling and elaboration of instructional language

One of the major challenges facing children on their entry to school is to develop fluency in school uses of language. Strategies for enhancing children's awareness of these uses, by planning their exposure to classroom language, have taken various forms. But a common feature in all has been the teachers' modelling of language requirements through systematic expansions or elaborations.

Instructional conversation

The so-called "instructional conversation" is one example of this. This procedure was developed from the experience of the Kamehameha Early Education Program (KEEP), and it has been applied in various settings. In one case, that of children from a low-income, non-English-speaking community in Southern California, the procedure was applied assuming that for these children schooling is synonymous with language acquisition.

The procedure involves the teachers reformatting both the instructional language that they use and their ways of interacting. Instruction includes deliberately activating the children's background information, directly teaching a skill or concept where necessary, and deliberately promoting complex language and expression by eliciting student rationales for their statements. Interactions include using fewer display sequences (where the teacher asks a question that they know the answer to), being responsive to children's contributions, and making connections across episodes of interactions between teachers and children.[8]

For example, in a lesson from a cycle of reading, writing, and discussion around the book *Charlotte's Web* (White, 1952), the teacher of a fourth-grade classroom systematically introduces themes, discusses relationships between terms, and develops abstract categorisations that are applied to the characters.[9] This is done in English with children in a bilingual transition programme. Concepts such as friendship and sadness, and being scared, characteristics that are alike or in opposition, and complexities in characters are discussed. The children and teacher immerse themselves in the concepts and terms.

The components of instructional conversation draw on and parallel components in other research-based programmes; for example, the Experience-Text-Relationship approach used in the Kamehameha programme. As in other procedures developed specifically for KEEP, the teacher employs a deliberate structure in comprehension lessons, with a "balance of rights" between the teacher's need to keep a lesson focus and the contributions that the children make. In this, as in other research accounts, there is evidence that this strategy is associated with higher levels of engagement in students and more complex language use by them.

Talkback elaborations

Instructional conversation as a procedure looks very similar to an "incidental teaching" procedure developed by Hart and Risley (1980) in early childhood settings serving economically poor communities with children whose English vocabulary was limited. It involved teachers systematically expanding on and elaborating children's utterances in shared activities and was used to increase the rates of growth in their vocabulary. However, in a more recent report, Hart and Risely (1995) have described how the rates of growth for these children over time are so much lower than for children from high-income communities that helping them to catch up poses an almost insurmountable task for teachers. This suggests that the systematic use of all the strategies discussed so far is necessary across both activities and curriculum areas within schools (not just during reading, for example) and across settings (to include families, for example).

There is research to back up this approach. Dickinson and Tabors (2001) report studies in Head Start classrooms with three- to four-year-old children from low-income families. The teachers' use of strategies that elaborated and extended children's language across activities in a variety of one-to-one and group situations was significant in enhancing literacy and language in kindergarten. Moreover, language interactions that extended and added new words at home further enhanced the teaching effects in the classrooms.[10]

Practice with perspectives and audiences

The third kind of strategy creates a bridge between the structured immersion strategies that we have just been dealing with and the strategies for explicitly priming awareness that follow. In the descriptions of classrooms that have created a community of learners for literacy, teachers and peers often act as an audience for children's writing or their reading.[11] This provides children with repeated experiences of taking different perspectives while responding to or acting as an audience. The process of shifting perspective between giving feedback on others' performance and receiving feedback on one's own contributes to the development of awareness and, in particular, the reflection on and control of language described in the previous chapter.

Dyson describes a third-grade group's performance of their written piece about X-Men in front of their classmates and the teacher. After the performance, the whole class discussed the piece, including questioning the author's decisions. Some participants in the discussion commented on and complained about author Sammy's text:

> *Michael: You just said "and the bad guys won." You didn't say which bad guys.*
> *James: The bad guys. You know, the bad guys.*
> *Michael: Yeah, but bad guys – what kinda bad guys? Are they mutants or not?*
> *Aloyse: Mutants.*
> *Michael: You don't know that.*
> *Aloyse: Were they mutants?*
> *Sammy: Yeah.*
> *Michael: You didn't say it in your story.*

After some more discussion, Kirsten, the teacher, comments, too:

> *Kirsten: I'd like to say that I was impressed with your story, that you were able to carry a story through and keep something else happening. To me, the* story *itself was* not *boring, whether or not Liliana herself got bored lying there [acting being dead] ....*

After further group discussion, Kirsten continues:

> *Have you seen a story where someone dies?* (general nodding) *It might be that a person who's acting in [the story] doesn't like it that they have to die, but is it OK for an author to make people die?* (general nodding)
> (Dyson, 1997, pages 120–21)

In this episode, the author has to reflect on others' perspectives as expressed through their reactions. It also shows the role of the teacher in mediating these responses – explaining and elaborating them. In this respect, the mediation functions both to teach the group directly and as a model for acting as an audience – in essence, teaching the children how to act as an effective peer group. Thus, the episode illustrates again the conditions described in the previous chapter – a community of learners in action. It also illustrates the role that the teacher plays in introducing topics and labels and concepts.

Priming awareness: the strategies for guiding reflection

Planned exposure provides children with practice *in situ*, enabling them to gain greater control over their understanding of language forms and uses in the classroom. But it is only half of what children who find schools risky places might need. Another of the rights for children that James Gee proposes is teaching that enables children to make sense of tasks in the classroom. This means the forms of guidance that focus the learner's attention on the language and practice that they need in order to be successful in the classroom. The attention to classroom tasks would produce reflection and an overall understanding of the patterns and relationships in the activities. This kind of priming of awareness is the basis for the three types of strategies that we explore later in the chapter.

Learning by imitation

There is strong theoretical support for the kinds of strategies in which teachers prime learners' awareness of tasks as well as enable their extensive practice of them. In Susan Blackmore's (1999) theory of imitation learning, she confirms the necessity of having extensive experience but adds an important rider to this. The learner imitates with greater accuracy, she says, if they have received instruction on and know the rules underlying the action to be imitated rather than just seeing its performance. When the basic format for a task has been made clear, through description and explication of rules, the learner is able to take into account the reasons for performing the activity or its goals. If the imitator is able to share an understanding about the goals, he or she can modify and regulate the performance of the task, concentrating on getting the important bits right and avoiding slavish imitation of unimportant bits.[12]

The less you know, the less you get of what you need to know

There is a further psychological reason for complementing the set of strategies for structured immersion. Without teacher mediation (which is typically present), such strategies would rely for their effect on the assumption that children will be able to spot the critical features of tasks through exposure to them. Immersion in repeated, rich, and varied activities carried out across varied settings would mean that the patterns defining rules for engagement would become obvious. But the insidious Matthew effects operate here, too. In complex cognitive tasks, the more one knows, the more one can pick up indirectly and incidentally. Thus, at school entry, the children who already know something about school tasks are likely to be better at picking out the bits that will enable them to know more.

In fact, it has been found that teachers in the early grades do not often instruct their children on the rules of engagement in classroom literacy activities through any form of deliberate guidance.[13] Furthermore, children of diverse cultural and language backgrounds tend to get even less direct instruction of this kind as teachers focus even more on teaching item knowledge for reading and for writing and, hence, exacerbate the Matthew effects.

Marking critical features and labelling

This strategy uses explicit reference and highlighting to enable children to become aware of the important parts of tasks, including the language involved in performing those tasks. In Chapter 6, we made the point that the tasks where this is particularly critical are those involving texts. There is plenty of evidence that it is possible and productive to develop children's letter–sound knowledge and phonemic awareness by explicitly marking letters and sounds for their attention and, under appropriate circumstances, for this to aid accurate and fast ways of decoding or producing words. However, there is a more pressing issue for teachers of linguistically and culturally diverse children – to identify strategies for priming the children's awareness of more complex language features. As we have argued in previous chapters, it is early and increased facility with texts that such children most need.

Contingent teaching

The effective use of this strategy in teaching younger children is marked by teachers using labels and terms contingently on children's responses. In this way, teachers clarify ideas in the reading and writing of texts. Kris Gutierrez (1992) provides an example from a class of Latino second- and third-graders, eighty percent of whom were monolingual in Spanish when they entered school. After a semester in this classroom, the students had better written and oral English-language skills than the children in other classes.

The classroom is described as a learning community, teaching being both responsive and collaborative, and also directed towards shared goals. This excerpt comes from one of a series of integrated lessons taken over several weeks on famous explorers. The students in the excerpt had negotiated a change in the form of an assignment – from narrative to expository. The teacher has already introduced the term "docudrama" but reintroduces it at the point where Roberto is trying to capture the concept:

Fran: Roberto, what are you doing? You write a book?

Roberto: I'm writing the best story ever. They're gonna make a movie from this one. Number one best seller.

Fran: It has to be true. Miss M says it has to be true and it has to be in the books. Don't forget.

Roberto: I didn't forget. It's true. I'm just making it kinda better. I told Miss M. She said it was a doc … [to the teacher]. What do you call it?

T: Call what?

Roberto: My story, my report, cuz you said I had some fiction. You know like they do on TV?

T: Oh a docudrama. I said yours was more like a docudrama cuz it was based on some facts.

Roberto: Yeah. I'm writing a do-o-c-u-d-r-a-m-a. I'm going to be like a famous television writer and make thousands, no millions of dollars.

T: Just remember our agreement. You have to be able to tell me and the class which part is true and which parts are made up. You have to know that. Also, we agreed that most of it had to be true. Did you figure out how you were going to let us know which parts are fiction?

Roberto: I'm gonna underline the parts that I made up. OK?

T: Oh, that's good. OK.

(Gutierrez, 1992, page 258)

Playing with language

An intriguing study is reported by Nicola Yuill (1996), who experimented with using unusual classrooms texts – jokes and riddles – to increase linguistic awareness. Understanding and appreciating riddles and jokes also requires metalinguistic awareness because it requires reflection on different uses of language. She reasoned that riddles and jokes require awareness at several different linguistic levels; for example, lexical (including awareness that words can have double meanings), syntactic, and functional.

Yuill provided a thirty-minute session once every seven weeks to small groups of children, some of whom had major problems with comprehension. The training included defining words with double meanings (for example, fan), inventing unusual meanings with word compounds (for example, sausage roll), and explaining jokes and double meanings. The seven-year-olds who received this training, both good and poor at comprehension alike, significantly improved their reading compared with a control group who had also had special sessions, in their case, reading amusing stories and receiving teaching on awareness of sounds.

The sessions with the awareness trainer (Kate) looked like this:

Kate: Sabine saw a man eating fish.
Kerry: ... and she wanted some ... and a fish eating a man.

Kate: Tell me how long cows should be milked.
Sabine: Until they are their normal size.
(Yuill, 1996, page 212)

The strategy in this form could easily be used with new entrants with diverse language and cultural identities. This would be especially so with children whose socialisation has included word and language games – in this way, the strategy would provide both incorporation and awareness.

Playfulness and awareness

Interestingly, playfulness with language as it arises within literacy activities, not necessarily programmed in a training sequence, is a feature in the activities of effective classrooms. It is also associated with effective intervention programmes such as Ann Brown and Annemarie Palincsar's programme of Reciprocal Teaching, discussed later in this chapter.

Palincsar herself (1993) reports an example with a teacher introducing a story about porcupines. The teacher began the dialogue, introducing the first of the strategies of Reciprocal Teaching, prediction. Palincsar's comments are interspersed:

Teacher: Our first story is called "The Porcupine". Now, we usually predict from the title don't we? So, obviously the story is going to be about – what Chris?

[One of the lessons one learns early in discussion with first graders is that there is nothing that is "obvious".]
Chris: A porcupine has a friend that's a cactus, and he has a girlfriend that's another cactus.
(Palincsar, Brown, and Campione, 1993, page 53)

Playfulness feeds into the development of awareness by enabling children to personalise an activity as well as by enticing them to become engaged in texts.

Directing attention to language uses

A second set of strategies specifically identifies ways of using language. These strategies extend the first set by focusing on how language functions as well as by adding terms and clarifying ideas.

Heath (1983) describes a classroom community in which children tape-recorded and analysed their own and their peers' language in such activities as storytelling or reporting. The second-graders became local ethnographers or, in the label adopted by the teacher, "detectives". They developed skills for looking at ways in which language, both written and spoken, differed across contexts. All sorts of people became resources, from the community as well as from the school (for example, the custodian) – they came to class to talk about their ways of talking and how they used written language, sometimes bringing samples. There was extensive use of a variety of texts, including excerpts from television scripts. The children learned to identify differences in formal and informal speech. For example, Heath records that they reported:

* *sounds that did not match those discussed in reading lessons (the dipthong /æh/ seemed "longer" in the speech of visitors than in the discussion of the sound for "long i" in phonics lessons);*
* *sounds that were discussed in reading lessons, but were not heard in some casual talk (final ng, final s);*
* *expressions not found in reading materials (ain't, yonder);*
* *words used in school written materials, but rarely used in talk (notice, instead of pay attention, this evening instead of tonight).* (Heath, 1983, page 329)

On some days, the children observed and recorded all the opportunities to use language (one day's total for the whole class was

15 528 different messages, ranging from the numbers on buses to commercials to library books). The class was known as the "readingest" class in the school. By the end of the year, they had developed a metalingustic vocabulary and ways of talking about their language and that of others. They could point out different levels of reading and different styles of writing and speaking for different purposes. They could identify and label and talk about dialect features and had developed definitions of literature types.

The children in this classroom (sixty-five percent white, thirty-five percent black) were from an impoverished mill community, many members of which qualified for social services. Of twenty-four students entering in grade two, eighteen were below grade level. On reading tests at the end of the year, fourteen students were reading on grade level, eight above grade level, and two below.

In this and other classrooms, Heath notes the presence of the conditions of a community of learners. This comment by a first-grade teacher captures how the children and teachers identify themselves as a group of learners with common purposes:

> *The psychological value of building positive self-concepts by having what could easily have become the "lowest reading class" become the school's prestige group is obvious. Carrying hardback readers and having homework each night from the first week of school gave the class an edge over other groups who had paperback primers and were not considered old enough for homework. Students learned to use the environment about them to recognise letters, to hear different kinds of questions and answers, and to talk about stories. In short, they came to see themselves as readers.* (Heath, 1983, page 287).

Explicit teaching of awareness and comprehending

The previous two sets of strategies enhance awareness by focusing children's attention on aspects of their own language. The first set identifies parts of their language or adds to them; the second set identifies the ways in which language can be used. The third set of strategies is an extension of the second. It focuses attention on ways of gaining meaning from texts. The clearest example from research of its effectiveness comes from studies of Reciprocal Teaching, a teaching procedure for comprehension strategies.

The Reciprocal Teaching procedure

Reciprocal Teaching has a well-developed theoretical rationale and has been extensively researched. The procedure is based on a shared text, read either as a readalong with the teacher, silently, or out loud, depending on the abilities of the children and the level of text. Four effective reading comprehension strategies were identified from experimental studies and descriptions of readers good at comprehension. They are:

- *predicting* upcoming content using prior knowledge and the text itself,
- *questioning* about content to stimulate discussion (may involve rereading),
- *summarising* to identify the gist and prepare for the next text portion,
- *clarifying* – used opportunistically to restore meaning.

A leader, initially the teacher but later each member of the group or class, guides a session, during which the teacher and the students take turns leading the discussion.

The teacher's roles include maintaining the "balance of rights" so that the group is kept on task. The teacher also provides the explanation, modelling, support, and feedback that enable students to participate and become leaders of the group. This is the important part of the strategy for our present purposes. Using the framework of co-construction, we can see the teacher's job as creating scaffolding of explicitly identified and shared ways of using the strategies with texts. The scaffolding is both direct and obvious. But it has other functions, too, linking contributions by members to new knowledge and reworking and elaborating contributions.

The procedure was developed with children from economically very poor communities who had been identified as needing remedial or intervention programmes. In one study with first-grade students, thematically linked expository texts were used. Five of the six children studied were described as at risk academically.

The following excerpt comes on the sixteenth of twenty consecutive days of instruction. The children are reading about the snowshoe rabbit. The segment of text already read was about the season in which the babies are born and ways of caring for them. This sample from the transcript reported by Palincsar shows the scaffolding and guidance of the teacher as well as their use of explicit labels for strategies (in bold) and the ways that they embed definitions and give models of what these mean.

Kam (dialogue leader): When [were] the babies born?

Teacher: That's a good question to ask. Call on someone to answer that question.

Kam: Robby? Milly?

Milly: Summer?

Teacher: What would happen if the babies were born in the winter? Let's think.

Several children make a number of responses including: "The baby would be very cold," "They would need food," "They don't have no fur when they are just born."

Kam: I have another question. How does she get the babies safe?

Kris: She hides them.

Kam: That's right, but something else ...

Teacher: There is something very unusual about how she hides them that surprised me. I didn't know this.

Travis: They are all in a different place.

Teacher: Why do you think she does this?

Milly: Probably because I heard another story and when they're babies they usually eat each other or fight with each other.

Teacher: That could be! And what about when that Lynx comes?

[discussion continues until ...]

*Teacher: So we agree that the mother rabbit uses her senses to find her babies after she hides them. Kam, can you **summarize** now?*

Kam: The babies are born in the summer ...

Teacher: The mother ...

Kam: The mother hides the babies in different places.

Teacher: And she visits them ...

Kam: To bring them food.

Travis: She keeps them safe.

*Teacher: Any **predictions**?*

Milly: What she teachers her babies ... like how to hop.

Kris: They know how to hop already.

Teacher: Well, let's read and see.

(Palincsar, Brown, and Campione, 1993, pages 47–48)

Part of the curriculum goal in these lessons was to produce analogies – drawing parallels between instances that illustrate the theme of the lessons. The data shows markedly higher levels of listening comprehension (recall, inferences, and understanding of themes). The children receiving the procedure were much better at drawing analogies from their original texts with assessment passages that had different themes from the original instructional passages. The children made connections between texts and across themes, not only within the experimental material but also with books and themes beyond those texts. There was no evidence of this awareness of text connections being present before Reciprocal Teaching occurred.

The strategies and text connectedness

What we have shown in this chapter is the presence of two complementary sets of strategies to enhance awareness so that children can unlock what is unfamiliar in the classroom. They are present in research that describes effective teaching with children who have minority cultural and language status living in poorer communities.

The evidence is that enhancing awareness of complex language forms and functions in classrooms at the beginning of formal instruction is possible. The first set of strategies is not just immersion in text activities. It is planned so that extensive and carefully orchestrated exposure across types of texts and across sites and settings can occur. Similarly, the second set is not just direct instruction of language forms and uses. It is deliberately teaching to prime children's understanding by marking features, identifying language uses, and directly modelling strategies for reading and writing. Both strategies are embedded in the use of texts. Both are dependent on (and contribute to) a community of learners. But if the teaching were detached from the use of texts, it could be predicted that the strategies would not solve problems for children and, indeed, could create added confusion.[14]

End Notes

1   Delpit (1995) argues for both these approaches. Although there are questions over whether the dominant discourse of the classroom is able to be learned by those outside that discourse, she provides strong evidence that discourses are permeable and learnable. She argues that to deny this availability is, at best, to patronise and, at worst, to create an insidious form of maintaining control.

2   The importance of practice receives widespread support in research evidence from other areas of learning. One example is Susan Blackmore's (1999) work on the significance of imitation in cultural transmission. Effective imitation involves decisions about what to imitate, it requires complex transformations from one point of view to another, and it requires the imitator to produce matched actions. The degree to which the imitator can achieve all these things depends on the complexity of the existing units of related imitation a person has, again derived from extensive experience.

3   Among those who have made this argument are Delpit (1995), Dyson (2001), Hemphill and Snow (1996), and Ladson-Billings (1994).

4   See Stanovich, West, Cunningham, Cipielewski, and Siddiqui (1996) and Stanovich, Cunningham, and West (1998), who make this claim after extensive analysis of developmental sequences and rates of acquisition under different text exposures.

5   The use of thematically linked expository texts with first-grade children occurs in implementations of Reciprocal Teaching, especially in science – see Palincsar, Brown, and Campione (1993). The use of these texts provides a basis for intertextual links, initially mediated by the teachers. This is a mixture of immersion and deliberate and explicit guidance, using the Reciprocal Teaching procedures.

6   Smith and Elley (1994) summarise a number of the studies in primary school, and Neuman (1999) reports a study with three- and four-year-olds.

7   See Ladson-Billings (1994), also referred to in Chapters 3 and 5. This is another "double-whammy" strategy in that it capitalises on both incorporation and awareness.

8   The concept of the instructional conversation is described in detail by Tharp and Gallimore (1988), who present it as a generic term for effective teaching and learning at many levels. Developments of the procedure have been described in a number of research reports by Goldenberg and others; for example, Saunders, Goldenberg, and Hamann (1992).

9   See Patthey-Chavez and Goldenberg (1993).

10   The research by Dickinson and Tabors (2001) adds to the evidence for the significance of structured immersion and embedded but explicit teaching. Their results show the powerful impact of language in early childhood settings on literacy and language development through such things as conveying information to talk about past, future, or hypothetical topics, analysis of text during book reading, talking about vocabulary (definitions and comments about sounds or functions of words), summarising extended chunks of text, clarifying comments, making evaluative responses to stories by both teachers and children, and extending utterances in free play (building on and extending what the child has said).

11   Heath (1983) describes classrooms in which children's oral storytelling and reporting are captured on tape recordings and written out. The effects of the peers as audience is through the editing of oral versions. Others have described classroom members reading and discussing each other's texts while the teacher also writes extensive reactions to texts. For example, the audience involved in "author's chair" or in performance of plays is extensively documented by Dyson (1997; 1999; 2001).

12   This is true for the studies of complex cognitive tasks in general (Siegler, 1991) as well as generalisation and transfer studies where greater transfer occurs with rule-based learning (Bransford and Schwartz, 1999). The corollary occurs in studies showing that learning without feedback on the accuracy of performance reduces generalisation and awareness (McNaughton, 1987).

13 In some studies, the incidence of direct instruction of strategies that might effect metacognition is as low as 2.3 percent of observational intervals (Baker, 1996).

14 As young children begin to develop expertise, it would be even more risky (even if it were possible) explicitly to teach for their awareness anywhere but within contexts where that expertise is best situated for high progress. Reflecting during the course of an activity provides the basis for awareness (Clay, 1999).

Chapter 8

Awareness and Reading Comprehension

Overview of the chapter

Focusing on text comprehension

Can teaching strategies be identified that enhance children's awareness of what to do in classroom activities? If so, how do they do it? The answer to these questions have been anticipated in the previous two chapters. With an appropriate set of curriculum conditions and with particular teaching strategies, children's awareness of what to do can be enhanced. This chapter explores the conditions and strategies in greater detail – as they relate specifically to reading comprehension.

In this chapter, we describe how all normally developing children on entry to school have knowledge and skills that provide a basis for text comprehension. We also show that, in the case of children from culturally and linguistically diverse communities, teachers can use the strategies for developing awareness – unlocking the unfamiliar – as well as those for building on the familiar to enhance the development of this expertise. Finally, promoting reading comprehension, particularly through reading to children, is discussed. This is used to extend the analysis of the acts of teaching that we used with phonics in Chapter 4, building a more complete model of teaching strategies in action.

Reading comprehension defined

Reading comprehension can be defined in a number of ways. The straightforward working definition is the "ability to answer reasonable questions about a passage one has heard or read" (Biemiller, 1999, page 6). This, of course, does not offer a definition of reasonable questions. A recent study of reading comprehension in some thirty countries did so by identifying the processes involved in answering the kinds of comprehension questions posed at school. These required children to:

- *retrieve* information explicitly stated in texts;
- *make inferences* based on texts;
- *interpret* and *integrate* ideas and information in texts;
- *evaluate text* by critically reflecting on and assessing content, structure, language used, and literary devices.

These processes serve a variety of purposes including reading for literacy experiences, and using information from across a range of texts.[1]

In addition, we can also define reading comprehension by identifying the strategies that children can use to produce these outcomes of retrieval – making inferences, interpretation, and evaluation. We discussed one such approach in Chapter 7 – that of Reciprocal Teaching. We can also look at the psychological processing mechanisms, including forms of monitoring and control, that underlie these strategies and outcomes. Our major concern in this chapter is the role of instructional strategies in effectively developing expertise in comprehending texts, given the various forms that this expertise takes at school.

The youngest age group in the international study was that of nine-year-old children. Are those same processes and strategies for comprehension applicable to children of the school-entry age group before they can read very much? We need to look at children of that age from a developmental perspective in order to answer this question.

The roots of reading comprehension at school

Reading comprehension does not start on entry to school. Ways of comprehending text have a developmental history starting long before school, arising out of family and community activities. Children's developing knowledge and skills can be plotted before school and over the period of transition to school. The presence of this expertise, as it relates to conventional comprehension of print in schools, can be easily demonstrated.

Firstly, we can look at the psychological bases for reading comprehension in the early years. These are forms of comprehension that are independent of any decoding of text. Listening comprehension, as measured by children's understanding of stories and expositions they have heard, is related to later reading comprehension. Children's receptive language and the size of their vocabulary provide a basis for developing comprehension, too. These two sets of relationships are strong. For example, a child's vocabulary size at the end of kindergarten year in the United States has been found to predict their reading comprehension measures up to seven years after entering school and, in one study, to predict about fifty percent of the variance in reading comprehension in the eleventh grade.[2]

Secondly, experimental demonstrations with preschool children show that children's listening comprehension before school can be advanced by particular ways of reading books to children.[3] What this means is that children's understanding of books can be systematically modified before decoding is learned.

Why are we waiting?

On the basis of this evidence, we do not have to wait for fluent and automatic decoding to be in place before teaching comprehension skills. This is not to deny the significance of fluent and accurate decoding. Its development is, of course, closely connected with reading comprehension.[4] The more fluent and rapid word recognition is, the more quickly it is possible to comprehend meanings of a specific text. But focusing on these features at the expense of attending to the development of comprehension creates problems. Again, the need for a balanced approach can be demonstrated easily.

We know that classrooms vary greatly in the amount of comprehension (including language) instruction that occurs but that instruction overall is probably insufficient for optimal literacy instruction.[5] Furthermore, we know that children of diverse language and cultural backgrounds are particularly vulnerable in their acquisition of these elements of conventional classroom literacy.[6] Classrooms in general do not provide the richest instructional conditions that they could early enough to enable these children to learn what they need to learn. The aim is to have instruction that sets children on an upward spiral of self-sustaining development. But this aim is less often reached for children with diverse language and cultural backgrounds.

The development of reading comprehension

Given the range of reading programmes available, and hence of channels for development, we would not expect to find a simple uniform progression in the development of comprehension. Hardly any kind of development works in this way, even motor skills.[7] But there is some consensus over the general picture of how conventional print skills develop over time and how comprehension skills develop within this.

Interlocking expertise

Grover Whitehurst and Christopher Lonigan (1998; 2001) have proposed a model for reading that distinguishes two sets of knowledge and skills. One set operates in the domain of language and knowledge – those concepts a child comes to have about the world, including their experiences in familiar events. The other set includes those processes that help a reader to decode print into sound and sound into language. For young children, both sets fluctuate in significance as platforms for further development in response to the guidance and instruction available in family, early childhood, and early school settings (kindergarten and grades one to three).

Expertise in representing events and ways of acting

The first of these two sets of knowledge and skills includes knowledge about the world and the vocabulary that one has to represent that knowledge. It includes conceptual knowledge about events and scripts for ways of acting and, specifically in literacy, ideas about different types of text structure. This set of knowledge and skills enables children to construct ideas about literacy and ways of using writing. Its presence is a strong predictor of early progress in school literacy. It also enables children to engage more effectively in teaching and their teachers to teach them more effectively in early childhood and beginning school – teachers and children, in this sense, are better synchronised.

Expertise in decoding

The second set, as it is evidenced in the early years before school, can be divided into three groups – print principles, writing skills, and linguistic awareness (including phonemic awareness). Children's development of knowledge and performance skills in each of these areas is related to their level of skill in decoding and reading accuracy in the beginning years at school. As formal instruction comes to focus on decoding – that is, accurately translating print into sounds and sounds into print – these skills, and the influences on them, become strongly predictive of further progress. They constrain the ongoing effects of the skills and knowledge that children have about their world.

The interplay between the two sets of expertise

But the knowledge and skills that a child develops for representing his or her world then reassert a special significance for further development as the decoding skills are solidified and become fluent and accurate. The early levels of vocabulary, as we have already noted, predict achievement comprehension as far out as grade eleven. The broader reach of this kind of expertise becomes even more important for further progress after that initial push of instruction on decoding. An extensive vocabulary, a well-developed understanding of the attributes of texts, and a knowledge of events that are related to the content of the school curriculum need to be developing to intersect with the narrower focus of decoding in order to build comprehension of texts as a whole.

Effective arrangements for balanced development

Different literacy programmes can shift around the relative contributions of these sets of knowledge and skills for further development. And this introduces a well-known conundrum. If one can arrange the channels for development in a variety of ways, on what basis can we decide the most effective arrangements? Whatever the arrangement, some shape to the development of literacy will emerge from children's measured progress in that programme, which can then be used as the yardstick for success in learning within the programme.

A solution to this conundrum was argued in the chapter on phonics. All other things being equal, an array of highly versatile activities should form the basis of a programme because more learning and better teaching for diversity are made possible within the breadth of scope such activities offer.[8] Furthermore, if activities offering a rich range of language uses are set aside or de-emphasised in the beginning years, two problems occur. The first is that sources for further language development are reduced. This makes it even more difficult for comprehension to develop and jeopardises rapid progress in literacy. A cap is placed on what would otherwise be a child's exponentially increasing access to the multiplicity of words, sentences, and types that feature in texts. The second is that integrated development is limited, thus slowing down development. Despite the finding that children can learn to read under different programmes, there are differences in rates of acquisition and generalisation.[9]

Some children, particularly those from culturally and linguistically diverse backgrounds, need to be able to unlock what might be unfamiliar about comprehending texts at school as quickly as possible, and instruction can make a difference. In the next section, we look at some examples of teaching strategies that can enhance children's awareness of what to do in comprehension and how to do it. We focus on one wide channel that is rich in possibilities for this to happen – the activity of reading to children.

Reading to children: a case study

Reading to children, as noted in Chapter 2, is an activity that can have multiple functions and serve multiple goals. Here we look at its capacity, as a means for creating awareness, to develop children's vocabulary and listening comprehension.

Before school

There are many studies, carried out in a variety of countries, that describe the effects of reading books to children.[10] In New Zealand, those studies show that reading to children is widespread at home, although there are differences between families in the frequency of reading, in the types of books read, and in the ways in which reading takes place.[11]

Expertise associated with styles of reading aloud

Three styles of reading have been described, constituting three different forms that the activity can take. These styles are not necessarily used exclusively – even during one session with the same book, families can switch with "textual dexterity" between styles to meet different purposes. In one, called a "narrative" style, the child and reader are often focused on meanings in the text. In the case of stories, this is the unfolding of events, the development of characters and their roles, and the relationships that the text has to life. The interactions are like conversations during which the reader provides scaffolding that guides the child into understanding and even debating text meanings. A second style, called "performance", involves patterns of modelling and imitation, through which the child is enabled to recite parts or even all of the text. The third style, called "item learning", is concerned with displays of knowledge of items such as colours, letters, or labels, and the interactions have a characteristic question, answer, and evaluation format. Skills in identifying items, as well as specific knowledge of them, are achieved through questioning routines initially controlled by the reader.

These styles are used by many New Zealand families, including indigenous Māori and Pākehā (of Anglo-European descent), and first- and second-generation Pacific Islands families. The studies show that when storybooks are the vehicle and children are three and four years old, Pākehā families tend to use the narrative style; other families, particularly Pacific Islands families, tend to use the performance style more often.[12]

Over time, and with familiar books, these styles provide activities that develop particular sorts of expertise. The narrative style, for example, is associated with comprehension strategies similar to those valued at school. The performance style is associated with (among other things) recitation memory. The item learning style, particularly with young children, is associated with learning about referents and referencing. What the studies show is that families can read books to children for different purposes and with different outcomes. The purposes include the specific things that children might learn to do, but they also include deeply important messages to children about what texts are for, what authority texts have, and how relationships in a family are expressed.

At school

We might expect that the variety of ways of reading to children for different purposes before school would be matched by a similar variety at school. Indeed, there are a number of studies of early childhood teachers and teachers in the early grades in primary school that show this. They do not show quite as wide a variation to suit different cultural purposes as might happen in homes, but they do show variation in components of the narrative style and in the focus of questions in the item learning style. This is not surprising, given the more deliberate professional goals teachers might have. But if those goals are to include that of promoting children's comprehension, then reading to children can achieve this in several ways. Two examples are described here.

Word learning

One way to influence comprehension is to improve children's learning of words. This can be done by sheer exposure, by the teacher simply reading books to children. A recent meta-analysis (Swanborn and de Glopper, 1999) suggests that under natural reading conditions – that is, when children are required to do nothing other than read – students will spontaneously derive the meaning from and learn about fifteen in every one hundred unknown words that they encounter when reading. This rate varies, depending on the ratio of unfamiliar to familiar words in texts, the size of the child's vocabulary, grade level, and achievement level.

This is, in a sense, the default learning condition. Without any instruction other than reading for pleasure, children can work out the meanings of fifteen percent of the words that they encounter for the first time in print. But the rate increases if instruction is provided. It is possible for the teacher to add more and more instruction into the activity; for example, in the form of commentary on, questioning about, and demonstrations of word use before and after reading. With teacher input, particularly on how to use the context surrounding the words of the sentence or the paragraph, children learn significantly more words from their reading.[13]

A similar pattern occurs when teachers read to children. In the best of conditions – when appropriate texts are selected and when the teacher provides explanations of new words – studies have shown impressive gains in word learning.[14] In a frequently quoted study by Warwick Elley (1989), seven- and eight-year-olds learned an average of eight words from three sessions (giving a total of forty minutes of reading time) in a week. These effects were powerful. The gains occurred across all children, despite any initial differences in their known vocabulary.

These effects can be seen as powerful in another sense. They have been achieved in the context of large-group and whole-class instruction. However, there are some areas where more needs to be known. For example, there is little systematic research on what makes an effective book, and teachers can find it difficult to select appropriate books ahead of time. But the studies do indicate that children's familiarity with and interest in the topic, as well as the presence (in narrative texts) of humour and action, are important features.

Again, it is possible to add more and more teacher instruction into the activity. Again, this can be in the form of commentary on, questioning about, and demonstrations of word use before, during, and after reading. The teacher's role can be increased still further to direct identification and definition of words.

Elley's study involved an experimental comparison in the rate of word learning between children who just heard the text being read and children who heard the text and had a teacher define and explain the words. The teachers' behaviour was prescribed for the experiment – they explained words, provided synonymous phrases for unfamiliar phrases (for example, "important things to do" for "pressing engagement"), role-played ideas, and used illustrations. Without this instruction, the children's rate of gain in new vocabulary was about fifteen percent. With it, the rate more than doubled to around forty percent over all groups, and even the lowest achievement group gained more new words.

Word learning in early childhood classrooms

Elley's research involved older children, and the research on children's gains in vocabulary through reading has generally not involved children at the beginning of reading instruction. But even at this early age and stage, there are examples of effective instruction, not necessarily intended as such, in early reading that have similar features. In a series of studies with three- and four-year-olds in early childhood classrooms in the United States, David Dickinson has analysed patterns of teachers' interactions most related to word learning while reading to children.[15] These interactions are likely to involve considering characters in the texts, encouraging predictions and personal connections, and analysing vocabulary. They are mostly embedded in the text – that is, they occur when the need to clarify, elaborate, or highlight arises during the reading. The following interaction contains all these elements. After reading the sentence "the mother bird's soft down", the teacher paused and initiated a discussion about an unfamiliar word:

Teacher: What's "the mother bird's soft down?" Does anyone know what that is?

Child: It's laying down.

Teacher: Well, it's not laying down.

Teacher: They call it "against her down."

Teacher: The down are her feathers, her soft feathers.
Child: Cuddle, cuddle.
Teacher: They cuddle against her down, the down is her feathers.
(Dickinson and Smith, 1994, page 114)

The teacher's intervention here is contingent on the possibility that children don't know a specific vocabulary item – "down". The teacher's initial question has two functions. It is a device to check the children's knowledge of this word and the object category to which the word belongs (feathers). It is also a model for the child of a checking strategy – in this case, drawing attention to the need to know a word. An ambiguous or inaccurate response confirms that the word isn't known and provides a basis for further input, using the text itself as an elaboration. Again, this elaboration has two likely functions. It provides the information but also models how to search for and retrieve information about things contained in the text. This is followed by a statement – "the down are her feathers, her soft feathers" – which provides a specific definition of the word and also elaborates the scope of a generic category (feathers include these types – soft ones called "down").[16]

The interaction is again a compelling demonstration of the multiple functions of "reading to" as an activity. Opportunities for learning have been created not only for vocabulary acquisition but also for concept learning and ways of using texts to search for and retrieve information.

Understanding texts

The patterns of interaction affecting listening comprehension can include ways of rehearsing the sequence of a narrative that has been read, or the details of an exposition. In another example from Dickinson's studies, the teacher (not the same one as reported above) reopened the book after reading it and initiated the following interaction.

Teacher: What was the boy looking for?
Child: His glove.
Teacher: His mitt, his baseball glove or his baseball mitt.
Teacher: So where did he look first?
Child: Up in the treehouse.
Teacher: In the treehouse, under the stairs, in the dog's ear.
(Dickinson and Smith, 1994, page 114)

Here too, the teacher's contribution has many possible functions. These include identifying a central theme, clarifying vocabulary, establishing the idea of narrative sequence, and modelling how a retelling might rehearse that sequence.

In this study, the overall style of talking with children during book reading and other classroom activities was associated with both word learning and understanding of story structure. Using this style was associated with higher receptive vocabulary a year later in kindergarten grade. Longitudinal follow-up of the children showed that the size of this vocabulary was a strong predictor of reading comprehension scores five and eight years later.[17]

Spin-offs for writing narratives

This relationship between reading to children and vocabulary development and reading comprehension is impressive. But, additionally, this style of interacting while reading to children in books, as well as talking in other settings, was found to have an effect on the quality of children's narratives. The researchers studied this by having the children tell a story about a sequence of pictures and then assessing how well their story was organised, how many elements of a story it contained, and how complex its syntax was. In turn, the quality of children's narratives was associated with the children's progress in reading at school – in Dickinson's and Tabors' studies, this meant significant relationships with reading comprehension at grades four and seven.

Explicit teaching and self-regulation

The level of teachers' contribution to the activity – essentially, the degree to which they work in explicit instruction – can go from the embedded format of the previous examples to direct instruction on how features of texts work and what strategies to use for comprehending. Several research programmes have provided evidence that comprehension strategies can be directly taught to first-grade children from diverse cultural and linguistic backgrounds. While these programmes differ in some detail, in all of them there is some specification of tasks and identification of strategies to perform them.

Evidence for this comes from an extensive study of first-grade teachers exemplary for promoting literacy in their classrooms compared with other teachers at the same schools (Pressley, Allington, Wharton-McDonald, Block, and Morrow, 2001). The teachers' selection for the study was by nomination from administrators, who used test scores and parental perceptions as their points of reference. The selection was validated in the study by students' achievement test data, reading levels and quality of writing and from researchers' observations of levels of engagement. These were clearly thirty very effective teachers.

Despite many differences in these teachers' programmes, there was a set of eight features common to all. Two among these are particularly associated with the use of awareness strategies. Firstly, skills were explicitly taught, mostly in the context of real reading and writing tasks, and not only decoding skills but also comprehension skills. Secondly, children's self-regulation was encouraged – in what to do, how to check, and how to reflect on tasks. These features can be seen at work in the following notes, made during observation of a teacher in a suburban school with a culturally and linguistically diverse population.

Pat wanted her students to become aware of how detail adds interest and makes a story easier to visualise and, consequently, to understand. Therefore, she modelled awareness of detail by thinking aloud while reading and writing. Stellaluna (Cannon, 1993) was read aloud when the children were studying bats. After reading, "Down down she went, faster and faster into the forest below," Pat asked the children to show her by using their hands how Stellaluna fell. "Yes," she said. "If the author just wrote 'She fell down,' we would not have known that she was falling very quickly." We observed Pat to refer to detail and its ability to enhance comprehension many times throughout the day while reading and writing with the children in a variety of contexts. (Morrow and Asbury in Pressley, Allington, Wharton-McDonald, Block and Morrow 2001, pages 191–192)

The researchers refer to this as a mini-lesson. These were frequently observed happening in the classrooms of effective teachers, often as an extended commentary or interaction contingent on an event within an ongoing activity. In this case, it was elaborating ideas about detail in writing.

Talk across activities: gluing a community together

Analysis of the teachers' language in the above studies illustrates a further requirement of awareness strategies if comprehension is to be fostered. The use of these strategies in reading to children promoted the development of vocabulary and comprehension. But the full power of these classrooms as developmental sites for vocabulary development and comprehension was only realised in the language used across a wide range of activities and settings. It was to be found in small group settings of book reading that entailed the talk that analysed texts, as described above. It was also to be found in large group settings where information was conveyed and talk about past, future, or hypothetical topics occurred. It was to be found during children's free play as teachers happened to build on and extend what a child had said. It was to be found, also, when teachers used new words and exposed children to rarely used words across all these settings and activities. The combined effect had a major impact on emergent literacy, receptive vocabulary, narrative production, and story comprehension.

At its most effective, the activity of reading to children does not exist in a vacuum – it resonates with other activities. We argued in the previous chapter that the effective literacy classroom has the characteristics of a community of learners. The teachers' use of language across all activities and in all settings is part of the glue that enables the community to function. The effectiveness of the interactions within the activity of reading to children is determined, at least in part, by the degree to which there is generalised, repeated, and varied practice across activities in how to use language.

Getting the balance right in the classroom: a summary

What does this view of learning comprehension imply about effective ways to teach? In this last section of the chapter, we review what we have said about teaching comprehension, through the medium of reading to children, to highlight the qualities and types of teaching that can be effective. This leads to an elaboration of the types of teaching acts that we introduced in Chapter 4.

Teaching with a well-balanced tool

In the classroom, activities are the vehicles for making teaching and learning happen. In literacy activities, written language is used as a tool to achieve certain purposes related to acquiring literacy. In the case of reading to children, the tool is embodied in the book that a teacher uses for reading to children. Selecting texts appropriate for young listeners presents teachers with a balancing act similar to that of selecting appropriate texts for instructing beginning readers.

Texts for listening that optimise opportunities for comprehension and word learning need to have a balance of familiarity and novelty in words and topics, both within and across the books selected. They need to match children's oral language in words and content sufficiently to guarantee "engagingness" and, at the same time, to provide sufficient opportunities for children to encounter new words, new meanings, and new topics. So the teacher's selection of such texts – as it were, acquiring a well-balanced tool – is the initial stage of getting balance overall in the approach.

Balancing the amount of support to give

Then there is the balance to be achieved in the amount of support provided by teachers. As we can see from the previous discussion, teachers' mediation can be worked into an activity like reading to children to provide varying degrees of support on which to build greater expertise. But the relationship between a child learning from that mediation and the amount of mediation is not necessarily straightforward. This is because the effectiveness of a teacher's comment, explanation, or elaboration depends on the level of expertise of the child or children with whom they are interacting. So a simple formula for how much support to add cannot be provided – more support (or less) does not necessarily mean better teaching.

The support that the teacher provides is, in effect, the teacher taking over some of the responsibility for expert performance of the tasks involved, in this way enabling the learner to achieve the goals of the activity. The wherewithal for expressing this support lies in the teacher's language in interaction – both to scaffold the children's performance within the activity and, through this, to provide a basis for them to know more and perform more effectively. Thus, the teacher enables the children to be more expert than they otherwise would be in both knowledge and performance.

Effectiveness of support

Experimental research illustrates the degrees of support that are possible. Elley's study discussed above had short, simple phrases of explanation embedded in the reading. In another experimental procedure (Robbins and Ehri, 1994), kindergarten children listened to a story twice with a brief introduction and no discussion of word meanings. This resulted in the probability of children learning sixteen out of every 100 new words, which is similar to the average probability for learning new words from one's own reading. Another study in Israeli schools of reading to children with diverse cultural and language backgrounds added interactions before, during, and after book reading.[18] The interactions in these experimental classrooms produced increases in reading comprehension and the quality of narrative productions.

Reading to children has also been researched as a component of the more extended teaching procedure of shared book experience. In one study (Reutzel, Hollingsworth, and Eldredge 1994), this involved an introduction to the book and discussion about it, including predictions and discussion of the story throughout the reading. In subsequent readings, further teaching of print conventions took place, and children were able to take a "big book" version and read it themselves. The enduring effects of the platform of support created by the teachers' previous interactions can be seen in the children's comments as they choose a familiar text for the teacher to reread.

T: What do you like best about the story?

S: I like the rhyming.

S: She was surprised with a scar on her stomach [some students share orally their own scars].

S: I know which is Madeline [looking at the cover]. She's the smallest one. They are holding her hand. I like the part where they come into Madeline's room with solemn faces [Teacher and students dicuss what is meant by solemn].

T: I like the way the pictures point up.

(Reutzel, Hollingsworth and Eldredge, 1994, page 48)

Teachers' support and children's expertise

Expertise is made up of knowledge, strategic performance, and self-regulation. The effectiveness of the teacher's support is relative to a child's level of expertise in each of these areas. In some instances, direct identification of a word and its definition is as effective as prompting in helping a child to develop understanding from context. Different dimensions of texts require different sorts of interactions to support children's learning; for example, at the level of concepts in the text, the themes and arguments in the text, and the structure of the text.

There are also strategies associated with learning about things that are referred to in texts and the labels for these things. They include looking in a dictionary, asking someone more knowledgeable, or searching for embedded definitions or "generics" in a text.[19] So, strategies can be modelled, labels can be told, meanings can be elaborated. But working in support requires providing enough information to enable the child's internalisation of strategies to proceed, under their control, but not so much that internalisation is curtailed. And yet, when children do have strategies under control, having the teacher simply defining or labelling something may be the most efficient and effective way to get the information that the child needs.

Balancing explicitness with children's capacity to understand

Another element in the balancing act concerns the levels of explicit teaching. The balance here is in providing explicit descriptions of what to do and how to do it while bearing in mind what children are effectively able to understand at the very earliest stages of learning to read. This is before children have developed a great deal of expertise in decoding and when they have limited knowledge about reading for meaning.

Some procedures for the direct teaching of comprehension with children from diverse language and cultural backgrounds at this stage allow for considerable levels of support. In Reciprocal Teaching, for example, four sets of strategies – questioning, clarifying, summarising, and predicting – are identified and taught to the children. In a similar procedure, Transactional Strategies Instruction, the strategies taught include relating current texts to prior knowledge, seeking clarification, visualising events, summarising content, and generating questions and interpretations when reading.[20] In each case, there is explicit instruction of the strategies as well as modelling and further guidance as students read, along with systematic practice across different texts. Ultimately, learners take over the role of identifying and controlling strategies.

Expert decisions within a wide curriculum

It is possible, as the research evidence for these procedures shows, for teachers to introduce very explicit kinds of support in effective literacy instruction. Gee's arguments for children's rights to explicit instruction are supportable – but, we would add, in the context of a wide curriculum, where teachers are able to select a wide variety of texts and where they can make expert decisions on appropriate activities and appropriate levels of support in those activities. Moreover, all classroom activities should cohere in this way – they are linked by language, and language, as we have said, is the glue that holds together a community of learners. The question of what this might require of teaching expertise is the subject of the next chapter.

End Notes

1   Full details are given in *Progress in International Reading Literacy Study* (International Association for the Evaluation of Educational Achievement, 2000).

2   These relationships have been described by Biemiller (1999), Tabors and Dickinson (2001), and Stanovich, Cunningham and West (1998).

3   Studies described by Sulzby (1994) and Whitehurst and Lonigan (2001) show that children's comprehension of books is affected by specific patterns of book reading.

4   The close relationship between fluency and accuracy of decoding and comprehension is common sense – if you can not read a word, how are you going to understand what it says? But Adams (2001), Snow, Burns, and Griffin (1998), and others all describe how fluency and accuracy in reading connected texts is essential for developing the psychological processes involved in comprehension.

5   This claim comes from Biemiller (1999).

6   The programme of research by Dickinson and Tabors (2001) and the profile studies of children described in earlier chapters demonstrate that these children are particularly "at risk" in schools.

7   The phenomenon of multiple pathways to common developmental outcomes is present in such disparate areas of human development as sensorimotor development in infancy (Thelen, 2001) and the development of close relationships across the age span (Rothbaum, Pott, Azuma, Miyake, and Weisz, 2000).

8   Pressley (1998) and Biemiller (1999) offer similar arguments.

9   Some of this evidence is reviewed in McNaughton 1987.

10 See reviews by Bus (2001).

11 These are discussed in McNaughton (1995).

12 Qualifications need to be placed on these sorts of summaries. The variation within a cultural group in their uses of different styles can be greater than the variation between groups. But the studies indicate a tendency for Pākehā families to be more exclusive in their use of the collaborative styles and for Māori families and Pacific Islands families to be more dexterous by using different styles.

13 See Fukkink and de Glopper (1998).

14 Biemiller (1999) has reviewed a number of these studies.

15 See Dickinson and Smith (1993) and Dickinson (2001b).

16 See Gelman, Coley, Rosengren, Hartman, and Pappas, (1998) and further discussion in Chapter 9.

17 The measure of extended teacher discourse predicted about 41 percent of the variance in vocabulary scores after controlling for a number of factors. Kindergarten receptive language scores correlated 0.71 with grade 7 reading comprehension scores (see Dickinson and Tabors, 2001).

18 See Rosenhouse, Feitelson, Kita and Goldstein (1997).

19 See the discussion of the research done by Gelman, Coley, Rosengren, Hartman and Pappas (1998). There are two broad ways in which language uniquely conveys category structure. The first is through naming, which provides basic information to service children's intention to form categories ("That's a dinosaur"). The second is by expressing scope, which services children's intention to form categories further through provision of information about boundaries, the less obvious properties of a category on which children build their elaborated concepts. One linguistic form that is particularly powerful is called by Gelman "generics", which are essentially phrases carrying essential and enduring information (for example, "bats live in caves"). Nouns turn out to be more important than verbs for this kind of learning.

20 See Palincsar and Brown (1984) and Brown and Campione (1994) for further descriptions of Reciprocal Teaching, and Pressley (1998) for Transactional Strategies Instruction.

Chapter 9

More on Being an Expert

Overview of the chapter

Teachers' expertise in creating awareness

This chapter extends the description of teaching expertise provided in Chapter 5 to deal with four key elements of the incorporation strategies that we discussed in Part Two, but thrown into sharper relief by the awareness strategies. These elements are:

* knowing what classroom activities require of children and teachers, especially the language tasks and texts that are the basis for literacy instruction;
* knowing how to use strategies effectively;
* being aware of "teacher talk" – the meanings of, and possible confusions arising from, instructional language;
* being able to build and participate in a community of learners who also happen to be teachers.

Shaky beginnings in developing expertise

In *Rousing Minds to Life* (Tharp and Gallimore, 1998), there is a case study of a first-grade teacher learning to use strategies appropriate for teaching reading comprehension lessons developed in the Kamehameha Elementary Education Program (KEEP). The programme aimed to create classroom comprehension activities with clear teaching goals and strategies that were culturally congruent with indigenous Hawaiian children.

Early in her in-service professional development, the teacher, Grace, introduced her first-grade class to the story of *The Billy Goats Gruff*. Her plan for the lesson was to identify the central theme of the story as the greediness of the troll.

Grace: Why, why, what was the problem with the troll?

Kanani: He wanted to eat ... He was greedy.

Grace: Greedy. Are you greedy?

Chorus: No.

Grace: What happens to you if you're greedy?

Louise: You going to come mean and you going to get spanking from your mommy.

Grace: Does the troll have a mommy?

Louise: No. [giggles]

Sheida: He's all by himself. He's lonely. He can't find an equal with nobody.

Kanani: His mom dies. He killed his mom.

Summie: He doesn't have food.

Grace: All right, so we know what we think ... You're thinking, that's your idea.

Kanani: He killed his mom.

Grace: He's that greedy and that mean? All right we learned something about the troll yesterday. We did find out one thing about him. What did we find out about him from our reading yesterday?

(Tharp and Gallimore, 1988, page 220)

The transcripts of her initial comprehension lessons contain few instances of the responsive teaching model that she and her mentor (a consultant for in-service professional development) were attempting to hone. The core of the model is a set of repeated thematic routines described as a three-part Experience-Text-Relationship (ETR) sequence. The first part of the sequence involves calling up prior knowledge and children's experience relevant to the text (E). This is followed by reading the text (T) and then drawing out relationships between the two (R).

The sequences depend for their effectiveness on the teacher's questioning and the responsive way in which the teacher incorporates and builds on the children's responses to the questions. This requires flexibility during the exchanges as well as the maintenance of goals for the discussion overall. Ideally, a transcript would show conversational exchanges that are clearly linked, developing both the theme – in this case, of greediness – and the children's response and connecting further with the children's ideas of meanness and family as they might relate to the text. In this transcript, there is little elaboration and there are changes of topic.

The difficulty that this particular teacher has in accepting the children's responses and building on them, the authors (and the teacher's mentor, a senior teacher) point out, comes from a limited knowledge of content. In this case, a lack of consideration of the literary qualities of even simple primary texts means that the teacher does not anticipate the kinds of discussion that the topic and the text could provoke. She is not prepared to respond by considering alternative interpretations of the text; for example, about sharing resources and territoriality. She does not recognise the possible readings of this book and, as these and other transcripts show, is somewhat confused by and dismissive of the "off the wall" comments from the children. Over several professional development sessions, the teacher's mentor enables her to start developing her skills for analysing plot and theme as well as those for building on responses and for her "in flight" regulation of interactions.

This description of one teacher's initial difficulty and her mentoring illustrate at least three of the elements of the expertise that awareness strategies require: awareness of what to teach, of how to teach, and of shared talk. We discuss these and the fourth, participation in a community of learners, in the following sections.

Awareness of what to teach

Teachers need to be fully conversant with all aspects of the activities they select, arrange, and use in the classroom, including the purposes for and uses of the language that are required to perform the activities. This understanding of language informs the strategies described in Chapter 7 and extends the idea of awareness of diversity. That is, teachers need to know the differences between classroom language as it is used and written, and the community languages of the children.

All-round awareness in "cultural modelling"

Carol Lee's procedure of "cultural modelling", described in Chapter 3, provides an example of the kind of awareness in operation. Cultural images are used to prompt children to share their language with the teacher. That shared language is then crafted into written language for the classroom.[1] This procedure requires particular knowledge from the teacher. It needs careful analysis of the classroom task; for example, of written narrative. It needs knowledge of what makes a good narrative in the various senses in which that term is used in school, so that, in this respect, the teacher needs to know a lot about literature of the kind valued by schools.

But this knowledge needs to be complemented by an awareness of the ways of using language and making texts that come within the cultural experiences of the students. In the case of African American students with whom Carol Lee and her students work, these are the language traditions of African American students in general.

From this range of knowledge, a teacher using Lee's procedure can then extract elements common to both school-based and cultural-based tasks, and, in the course of teaching (as we shall see later), act to promote children's awareness through their reflection and control over both kinds of tasks.

For example, a particular teaching sequence uses illustrations of well-known historical and contemporary African American scenes.

Teachers use these scenes with their African American students to elicit what Lee calls a general cultural script – ideas that express meanings about such situations common to the communities that the students come from. A scene may also elicit more personal scripts involving individuals' specific experiences of such situations. This sets off a class discussion mediated by the teacher, who writes up and displays the students' vocabulary and phrases.

Awareness of the requirements of classroom language

Teachers must be aware of the properties of the oral and written language needed in classrooms if strategies to develop children's literacy are to be successful. In beginning literacy instruction, this means knowing what the structural properties of different texts might be; for example, the ways narrative texts can vary and how they differ from expository texts. But it also means knowing what is required when the text is used in a particular activity. For example, as we noted in the previous chapter, reading to children can be performed using different styles. These styles create different forms of the activity with different outcomes. If the purpose is reading to comprehend narratives, then an awareness of effective configurations to achieve this is needed. Lack of such awareness is why some ways of reading to children in classrooms are likely to be confusing or may even undermine children's development of ways of comprehending.[2]

Awareness of types of writing and texts

How do teachers develop this necessary awareness of types of writing and types of texts? Christine Pappas (Pappas and Zecler, 2001) argues strongly that teachers, like children, need immersion in the written word – extensive exposure to and practice with a wide variety of texts – both during their initial training and further professional development. In her professional development programmes, Pappas gets teachers specifically to seek out and articulate similarities and differences in diverse types of books, including the many that do not fit easily into a simple genre categorisation. (There are hybrid books for beginning instruction that blur distinctions between expository and narrative, just as children create written texts that are hybrids.)

This awareness does not just apply to texts, though. Everything that has been argued here also applies to the coded components of written language that children need to learn, including the structures of the sound and alphabetic systems found in it. Teachers need to know about these properties of language so that they can monitor and build on children's knowledge of them.

Awareness of how to teach

The second element of expertise is awareness of how to use strategies effectively – often called procedural knowledge as distinct from propositional knowledge (knowing the content of what to teach). As we have seen in the discussions about phonics and comprehension, awareness of this kind shows itself in the balance of flexible and adaptable uses of teaching acts within activities.

Awareness of overall procedure

The teacher who used the code-switching strategy for the comprehension of rap songs (described in Chapter 7) was aware of how she went about using the strategy and could explain her goals:

> We'll continue doing this kind of thing all year long. I want the children to see that they have some valuable knowledge to contribute. I don't want them to be ashamed of what they know, but I also want them to know and be comfortable with what school and the rest of society requires. When I put it in the context of "translation" they get excited. They see it as possible to go from one to the other. It's not that they are not familiar with Standard English ... they hear Standard English all the time on TV. It's certainly what I use in the classroom. But there is rarely any connection made between the way they speak and Standard English. I think that when they can see the connections and know that they can make the shifts, they become better at both. They're bilingual! (Ladson-Billings, 1994, page 84)

Awareness in particular interactions

This awareness at a general level is paralleled by awareness of how to proceed at more specific levels in day-to-day interactions with children. It is worth reviewing Susan Gelman's (1998) research to make the point. Her evidence is that children are very sensitive to the way that adults signal labels for objects and the categories into which they fit. Children learn to assign features to categories (for example, dogs have four legs and a tail, and they bark), partially through language, specifically through words that name and express the scope of categories (for example, in talking about a picture, "Look, there's the dog. I bet it's got a loud bark").

Caregiver talk

In a study of mothers reading to their two- to three-year-old children, the mothers used these "generics" quite frequently (three-and-a-half times per one hundred utterances in an expository-type book designed for the study). The evidence is that language that provides labels and categories in this way during reading is a powerful device for children's learning. These mothers (highly educated, middle-class women) seemed to use the procedure to enable their children to anchor the new words that they encountered in books. They were aware that they did this at a general level, seeing their reading to their children as a most important way for the children to obtain information as well as being important for their relationship. But it is questionable whether they were aware of precisely how they used "generics".

This is where the difference between family practices and the professionally based expertise of teaching at school becomes important. The actions of a teacher require a heightened and more detailed awareness of curriculum channels and moment-by-moment opportunities. Whether it is to expand or elaborate or name, the teaching act needs, as much as possible, to be under conscious control.

Awareness of performance

Expertise in teaching, as in other fields, includes the ability to modify performance. For teachers, this means adjusting instruction according to circumstance even when – despite the effectiveness of the curriculum, the selection of activities and the strategies used – instruction does not go right. A telling example of adjusting actions when a teaching act has not

worked or is not on the right track is contained in the following interactions
recorded with children nearly five years old in a kindergarten (originally
discussed in Chapter 2).

Episode One

*Text (teacher reading): The bear couldn't believe his ears. He gulped and sniffed
and wiped his tears. "You can talk after all," he cried.*

T: *He has got little ears hasn't he. Yes, he has got little ears, what about Eddy?*

C: *Big ears.*

T: *Has he not got little ears, what about you?*

C: *No, you have got big ears.*

T: *I have got big ears, yes, I know.*

C: *I have got little ones.*

T: *You have got little ears, yes dear.*

Episode Two

*Text (teacher reading): Don't be scared, you're my teddy. "No, I'm not," cried
the voice. "It's me, Eddy."*

T: *Look at the look on his face.*

C: *Aaaa big face.*

T: *Mmmmm*

C: *Big face.*

T: *Yes, he has got a big face.*

C: *A little face.*

T: *Little teddy bear.*

Episode Three

T: *Oh, what about this one here?*

C: *Big face, a fat face.*

T: *He looks a bit worried doesn't he?*

C: *This is a fat face.*

Episode Four

T: *What is he doing here?*

C: *Mmmm holding teddy.*

T: *He is holding his teddy. What is he doing with his other hand?*

C: *Scratching his nose.*

T: *He is scratching his nose.*

C: *Yeah.*

T: *I think it looks to me that he has his thumb in his mouth.* (Phillips, McNaughton, and MacDonald, 2001, 67–69)

In the first episode, the teacher asked a question in keeping with an item learning style of interacting (employing questions that ask children to display their knowledge). This style had been a typical practice in this kindergarten, particularly focusing on adjectives of colour, shape, and size. The teacher, however, had been participating in professional development that emphasised using the narrative style of interacting when reading this kind of rich story text to children. Her display question, though, was not directly related to the complex themes of loneliness and making friends arising from the text. It did not directly activate the children's own experiences to understand the characters or events in the narrative.

Understandably, given the style of reading that they had been used to and the interaction in the first episode, the children picked up on the comparison between big and little as the reading went on. But in episodes Two, Three, and Four, the teacher continually redirects their attention to aspects of the text that will lead to a discussion of the story's theme (the look on his face in the illustration, being a bit worried, and sucking his thumb).

Missed opportunities can be obvious with hindsight. In an analysis of the transition of Māori children to school (Turoa, 2001), one of the children had difficulty engaging with school activities. Hona, a new-entrant five-year-old, had been quiet and uninvolved during several sessions of observation. But in one activity, a story-reading episode in the first week at school, Hona's difficulty began to vanish.

Teacher: This story's about "Claire's Dream" … there she is [showing the front cover]. She's dreaming about something…. got her eyes open, but she's [day] dreaming about something. Or it's called "The girl who wanted to play rugby". [to the class] … Hands up those who like rugby?

Hona [calls out]: I play rugby!

Teacher [doesn't hear Hona].

Other children [call out]:…I like rugby….I play rugby

Teacher: Good. Hands down. [Begins to read the story]. "I'm going to be an All Black".

Hona [calls out]: I play rugby!
Teacher [doesn't hear Hona, continues reading to the end of story...]
(Turoa, Wolfgramm, Tanielu, and McNaughton, 2002, in press)

The selection of an appropriate text, the topic of which was likely to be familiar to several members of the class, had the desired effect. But the opportunity to draw in Hona more directly by responding to his contribution – the first observed from this child in a classroom activity – was not acted on.

Awareness of teacher's talk and shared understanding

Expertise involves the teacher being aware of their own use of language for classroom communication as a potential problem for children. The children's problem lies not only in how the teacher uses language, as we have already noted, but in what that language actually means.

Gwenneth Phillips (Phillips, McNaughton and MacDonald, 2001) argues that teachers' language when instructing children inevitably creates difficulties of understanding because what is said is not transparent, especially to a child new to learning tasks.[3] A child's understanding of a teacher's question or comment depends on three things. One is the meaning taken from the words and syntax – what is said. One is the meaning taken from the semantic intent – what is meant. There may not be a direct relationship between the two. A third is that both of the previous two depend on what Phillips describes as a set of presuppositions held by language users. The presuppositions are grounded in the activity in which the users are engaged. These presuppositions provide a basis for searching out what is meant, and they signal what is relevant to be considered.

Figuring out instructional dialogues

At the early stages of instruction, children and teachers may have different presuppositions about what is said and what is meant, and so each may fail to figure out what the other means or understands. Phillips gives an example where a teacher is taking a running record. The book is ready, as is the teacher, who thinks that the child is ready. The teacher says, "Off you go" – and the child gets up and leaves.

Phillips's analyses have various implications for looking at the meaning of instructional language. For example, if teachers and children are to come to share the understanding of a task, teachers need to select activities that are meaningful and authentic (as described in Chapter 6) and to incorporate instructional dialogues within them. These kinds of problems and their solving provide a window for both learner and teacher to see each other's presuppositions. In core reading and writing activities, the teacher needs to help the child to see the relevance of the child's existing knowledge in relation to what the task requires. For children with less control over English vocabulary and structures, the instructional dialogue (if it is in English) becomes a means of providing children with the language needed in the activity. The goal of instruction needs to be kept clearly in mind – the development of children's self-regulated activity through co-construction.

Questions, prompts, directives, and comments

For the teacher, specific teaching acts – the questions, prompts, directives, and comments – need to be consistent, contingent, and used with clear intent. Take, for example, a prompt of the following sort when a child miscues during instructional reading: "Try that again and see if that makes sense" or "Does that make sense?" Teachers need to be aware why they might use such a prompt. In professional development sessions, Phillips asks teachers to reflect on what they are helping the learner to do, what aspect of critical behaviour they are supporting, and how this helps the child with the search for what is important in the task. Teachers' awareness needs to extend to knowing whether a child is going to know what such words as "that" or "sense" refer to.

Their awareness should allow for consistency, contingency, and clarity across similar events in various activities (for example, similar miscues), as well as across various tasks requiring similar processes (for example, reading and writing). In writing, for example, a teacher might say, "What letter would you expect to see?" to get the child to focus on sound-to-letter relationships, and the prompt could be used for the same purpose in reading.

Phillips's professional development has been used in a very successful intervention programme for Māori and Pacific Islands children in economically poorer communities in New Zealand.[4] The degree of success was determined by whether the children's achievement in literacy after one year, across twelve schools, could be raised to come within national expectations. This result was generally achieved, not only in aspects of item knowledge but, most importantly, in levels of text reading and writing. Figure 4 in Chapter 4 shows these results.

Issues of awareness in diverse classrooms

How can teachers of children with diverse cultural and linguistic backgrounds have these kinds of awareness about all the members of their classes? How, for example, is a teacher able to have the in-depth knowledge illustrated by Carol Lee's cultural modelling approach when there is a variety of cultures, a variety of language traditions, and a variety of cultural scripts as well as personal scripts represented in the classroom?

Drawing on sources offered by the child, family, and community

In the earlier chapter on expertise, we described how teachers depend on three sources – the child, the child's family, and the child's community – for developing awareness of diversity and of those experiences of language and literacy that are common to communities and families. The further knowledge that the strategies for developing awareness require can be illustrated again, using these sources.

Popular culture

In a multicultural society, there are certain shared scripts (knowledge of patterns of events and characters) with which many families and children across all communities are familiar. In urban New Zealand, for example, these include those centred on sports, similar urban settings (often including proximity to beaches), television series, films, and, increasingly, the use of the Internet and electronic games.

Evidence for the pervasive presence of experiences common to all children in urban settings comes from Dyson's (1997) studies of children's writing. She has tracked the sources of texts created by children from their knowledge of sports teams and popular songs gleaned from television, radio stations, family members, and peers, as well as their knowledge of stories and characters from television series and films. The subtitle of her book *Writing Superheroes* is "Contemporary childhood, popular culture and classroom literacy". Her argument, backed up by a plethora of classroom examples, is that popular culture is indeed popular and is part of the scripts common to children in a local urban community.

For Dyson to accomplish this work, she had to understand both the sources and the characteristics of the children's writing. She had to act somewhat like an anthropologist in probing for the sources of children's knowledge. This meant tracking references and interviewing insiders to events, such as the personnel at radio stations and the members and managers of sports teams. Clearly, the scope of Dyson's work is beyond what a teacher might do. But the stance is something that a teacher can achieve.

The ethnographic stance

Being able to understand the nature of children's uses of language and the sorts of literacy activities with which they are familiar requires something like an ethnographic stance. In earlier chapters, we have shown how teachers can learn to act as ethnographers in their own homes and workplaces, observing and describing activities involving ways of learning and using language. This has enabled them to reflect on their beliefs, the nature of their own uses of language, and their knowledge of classroom tasks. The evidence is that the systematic use of children, families, and communities as a resource enables teachers to develop their awareness of dialect variations and practices and the ways in which classroom texts are the same as or different from these.[5]

A community of teacher learners

Teachers do not have to act alone to develop their expertise in awareness strategies. They are part of a community of experts with whom they work. We have seen how a community structure can create more opportunities for learners to incorporate their expertise in, and to develop their awareness of, what is needed for effective reading and writing. This can occur through direct and indirect forms of exchange between members of the community. The patterns of their interactions heighten awareness of tasks – this is particularly significant for children, given that the nature of expertise in contemporary literacy requires forms of teamwork.[6]

The pooling of expertise

Teachers, too, can view themselves as communities of learners with the explicit purpose of capitalising on their various talents in order to provide multiple "ways in" to effective teaching with children in diverse urban schools. Indeed, to paraphrase Ann Brown's quote in Chapter 6 on communities of learning, it would be a worthy intention to increase diversity and non-conformity in the distribution of expertise and interest so that everyone can benefit from the subsequent richness of available knowledge. The essence of teamwork is pooling expertise.

Teachers can work in their classrooms in relative isolation from other teachers. It is possible to be effective with little reference to other experts. But expertise could be enhanced by the sense of teamwork suggested by Brown. The diversity of team members could add to the expertise of the individual – it is extremely difficult for one person to have detailed knowledge of diverse communities, texts, and language practices as well as to have at their fingertips contemporary developments in theorising and research about language and literacy.

This knowledge can be held and developed within a group of experts. Their very diversity will provide the basis for a more elaborated and dynamic form of knowledge than that of a teacher acting in relative isolation. What does it take? Barbara Rogoff's analysis of communities gives some defining characteristics:

> A community involves relationships among people based on common endeavours
> – trying to accomplish some things together – with some stability of involvement
> and attention to the ways that members relate to each other. (Rogoff, Turkanis
> and Bartlett, 2001, page 10)

Cultural practices in a community of professionals

A community develops a set of cultural practices – cultural in the sense that Rogoff considers the practices to be shared and dynamically related, co-ordinated over time, and adaptive to new challenges and circumstances. The practices include ways of dealing with conflicts and crises. They also involve ways of celebrating success and new developments. The relations between members are multifaceted and take different forms, depending on purposes. The need to get a job done is not the only pattern of relationship – there is also the need to relate and resolve problems in members' practice and to maintain the cohesion of the group.

History and transitions

Another characteristic of a community is its history across generations and its development of ways of handling transitions from generation to generation. This is especially significant for schools where teachers and parents have limited periods of time acting as part of that community. The idea of cultural practices can be extended further. A community is dynamic, maintaining core values while adapting to change and experimenting with new ideas. Rogoff argues that this concept is inconsistent with the idea that forming a community involves applying a recipe of techniques to a new collection of people:

> *It requires the participation of the people involved in inventing and adapting customs and traditions, who learn from their efforts to develop the principles and practices for themselves.* (Rogoff, Turkanis, and Bartlett, 2001, page 10)

The cultivation of expertise

In classroom communities such as those described by Brown and her colleagues (see Chapter 6), the distribution of expertise does not occur by chance. It is deliberately brought about through particular activities. Examples include co-operative learning, where research groups working on subtopics need to pool their expertise to complete the full topic. The distribution of expertise also occurs incidentally as children "major" in particular facets of a topic and pursue these majors within the boundaries of the overall topic.

The community also develops through formats and familiar ways of participating practised by its members. For example, the forms of co-operative research have distinct structures and become familiar. Discourse in which constructive discussion, questioning, and criticism are familiar and expected is central to the community. The "seeding", "migration", and "appropriation" of ideas – how members exchange ideas, vocabulary, concepts, and methods – are common phenomena. These, too, are all features needed in a community composed of teachers who learn from each other.[7]

Research and development

Besides all this, teachers need to have access to professional knowledge that can be shared.[8] Even as a community, they may struggle to develop the knowledge they need to teach more effectively. Teachers and schools do not have a developed research infrastructure to create and share a lot of this knowledge. To meet this need, a second research system (complementary to the one in research-led institutions) is needed – one concerned more with identifying effective practices and with systematic replication of practices across groups of schools. The vision is to create purpose-built consortia of teachers and research colleagues – a community of learners with common issues and needs for knowledge.

On becoming and being an expert

We started the chapter with Tharp and Gallimore's description of a teacher developing awareness of her teaching and of the nature of effective classroom activities. We can end it with their note of warning. Their case study of Grace reveals:

> ... the complexity and difficulty to be expected when even a dedicated, able teacher attempts to learn responsiveness to children's ZPDs [zones of proximal development]. It took a wide range of assistance by the consultant, involving the full battery of means of assistance, and the creation of ad hoc activity settings. It required an extended, complex, sometimes frustrating instructional conversation. The sessions also reveal the joys accompanying Grace's achievements and the two women's pleasure in their developing intersubjectivity. (Tharp and Gallimore, 1988, pages 247–248)

Diversity in a community of teachers

The expertise of teachers and their teaching that we have discussed in this book so far has two main elements. One is the nature of expertise as it is enacted in the classroom. The other is the nature of learning – how one learns to be expert and to maintain that expertise. The term "expertise" has been employed here to describe the nature of teachers' relationships to both children and their field of professional competence. However, there is some antipathy towards the terms "expert" and "expertise" (Cochran-Smith and Lytle, 1999). New models of teacher education assume that, in the construction of a community for teaching effectively, the participants all function as fellow learners. The community may include teachers who are experienced as well as beginning teachers, and researchers as well as teachers. They may be "positioned" differently one from another, with different knowledge and experience, but they are not in expert–novice relationships with each other.

This misses an essential psychological characteristic of learning – that the features of one's performance as a professional are both personally and socially constructed. In this co-construction, there are forms of knowledge and of performance that are relatively more effective and more knowledgeable at both a personal and a collective level. The notion of culture and community can also be considered at both these levels. Being prepared to teach and learn from each other is part of this, and the meeting of minds in diverse classrooms can be built on diversity in the teachers' community, too.

End Notes

1   The children in Lee's studies of cultural modelling were older than new entrants, but the approach of cultural modelling illustrates the significance of awareness in the sense of knowing about tasks and how to use strategies.
2   Another example comes from Phillips, who points out that if the goal is to search for an author's meanings, the practice in some classrooms of trying to predict details of the narrative from the front cover before reading the book to children may not be a very effective way of using the text (Phillips, McNaughton, and MacDonald, 2001).
3   See Phillips, McNaughton, and MacDonald (2001).
4   See Phillips, McNaughton, and MacDonald (2001).
5   See classroom studies reported by Heath (1983) and Dyson (1999a) for this evidence.
6   See the quote from Brown on page 129.
7   Examples of these phenomena can be found in descriptions of effective study groups (for example, Dyson, 1997).
8   This argument is based on comments in Tharp and Gallimore (1988).

Part Four

PART 4

Great Expectations

Chapter 10

Efficacy and Excellence in Acquiring Literacy

Overview of the chapter

The energising effects of expectations of success

The previous chapters have described curricula and strategies associated with effective teaching for children from diverse cultural and language backgrounds. In each chapter, the point has been made that this effectiveness is not dependent simply on using any one set of strategies or putting in place any particular programme of instruction. When one observes mainstream schools that have achieved higher-than-expected success in literacy achievement – many serving the economically poor communities from which these children often come – there is not any one strategy or programme that stands out as the single cause. This last chapter is, in a sense, about what contributes overall to effectiveness – the energising beliefs and expectations that have perhaps been only hinted at in the analysis so far.

Snapshots of effective classrooms

An indication of the nature of these beliefs and expectations is captured in the conclusions of a large-scale study in 140 first-through-sixth-grade classrooms (Knapp, Shields, and Turnbull, 1995). The researchers observed and interviewed teachers, examined curriculum materials, spoke with children, and analysed daily teacher logs over a two-year period. The classrooms were in high-poverty schools that had achieved better-than-average results in academic achievement. Much of the description of classrooms identified as effective in literacy instruction should be familiar to readers by now.

The researchers found that teachers maximised children's comprehension by increasing the amount of time spent actually reading texts, by explicitly teaching comprehension strategies, and by providing opportunities to discuss what they were reading. Substantial time was devoted to the teaching of mechanics, too. However, learning was linked to the reading of texts and occurred within a wide range of tasks that engaged children in "making sense". The usual time allotted to writing was extended to cover a variety of types of texts, providing avenues of expression that the children in these schools had been often denied because of a focus, in conventional approaches, on basic skills before higher-level skills. The reading instruction enabled the children to get behind the literal meaning of words and seek deeper understanding.

A relentless focus on success

These descriptions resonate with what has been presented elsewhere in this book. It is the conclusion that is important to the focus of this chapter. The authors stated that the practices of the teachers in the schools challenged:

> ... the myth that, because of their presumed or apparent deficiencies in relevant skills, children in high-poverty classrooms should not engage in academically challenging work until they are "ready" – that is, until they have mastered all relevant basic skills (if that time ever arrives). (Knapp, Sheilds, and Turnbull, 1995, pages 7–8)

The teachers had high expectations of their children, a conclusion echoed by those from other research-based interventions in schools demonstrating high achievement in conventional literacy.[1] The details of literacy programmes may differ in some respects across the various models of programmes, and the dynamics of implementing the curriculum may vary, but a common core is the expectation that every child can succeed. The teachers are able to put into practice what has been called elsewhere a "relentless focus on the success of every child" (Slavin and Madden, 2001).

What high expectations mean

What helps teachers to have those high expectations of success? There are three closely related elements. The first is the beliefs, held personally and collectively in a community of teachers, that enable teachers to see their students as highly capable. The second is a sense, again both personal and collective, that the teachers can be effective, that they can recognise what resources are available for teaching and learning, both in and out of school, to enable children to realise their capabilities. The third is the setting and checking of high-level goals within the school community, including the skills for monitoring and evaluating personal and collective success. We shall examine each of these in turn.

Believing in success
Seeing children as highly capable

A strong theme runs through studies of effective teachers of various cultural groups in many different contexts. In addition to the strategies and knowledge we have discussed in previous chapters, the teachers have a characteristic set of high expectations about the capabilities of children.

Oral accounts by Māori adults recalling memorable teachers in New Zealand's Native Schools often make mention of these teachers' beliefs in what children could achieve – a sense of expecting a lot of children.

> *The teachers were good. They all tried to make us sit exams and scholarships and all that. They gave us extra tuition. The teacher we had when we were there was really good to all of us. Made us sit scholarships.* (Māori pupil, from 1945)

> *I reckon we had a very high standard at our Native School. I always maintain that the teacher who taught us was years ahead of the education system, and that's why we got so many people on scholarships year after year.* (Māori pupil from 1948 who became a teacher)

> *The most high, in my opinion, spectacular teacher was ... a Pākehā [Anglo European] fellow from Christchurch. He had just returned from one of the big universities in Oxford or Cambridge ... He came there with no concept whatsoever of dealing with or having anything to do with Māori before. But that didn't make a difference – he was such a genuine man. And with his arrival my interest ... soared. He introduced ancient history ... Roman history, which I found fascinating, and he got a library going for the children.* (Māori pupil from 1939) (McNaughton, 2001, page 93)

Not-so-great expectations

The range of beliefs about capabilities is illustrated in studies of teachers involved in professional development programmes aimed at helping them to lift the achievement levels of children in the economically poor urban schools that often serve communities of diverse cultural backgrounds. It is not uncommon to find that these teachers tend to attribute success or failure to variables of family background and other sociocultural features, and failure, in particular, to the economic and cultural (if not linguistic) deprivation that they see children from poor urban backgrounds as having. This is indicated in a typical comment from a teacher, before participating in such a development programme:

> *Some of these kids, their connections were never made when they were little and they can't be. If those neurons don't start firing at 8 months or 9 months, it's never going to happen. So we've got some connections that weren't made and they can't be made up.* (Betsinger, Garcia, and Guerra, 2001, page 25)

Teachers in such situations may defend their primary role as one of providing a caring and nurturing environment at the expense of academic instruction. Another teacher's comments put this tension succinctly:

> *What I've learned is that teachers are here to educate children to become meaningful citizens, productive citizens in society, but just from my experience with these children, that can't happen until they feel safe and comfortable and cared for …. It's very important to me that all of my children can read by the time they leave [this] grade and everything like that, but first and foremost when they come to my room is I want them to trust me and I want them to be comfortable.* (Betsinger, Garcia, and Guerra, 2001, page 25)

In another study of teacher beliefs about the abilities of children from poor communities on entry to school, teachers commonly expressed the view that, in general, these children, many of whom had English as a second language, had inadequate and inappropriate early skills. Examples that they cited included children eating crayons because they couldn't distinguish between them and food and lacked knowledge that crayons were a writing tool (Timperley, Robinson, and Bullard, 1999).

Explaining away low expectations

There is a parallel to teachers' attributing children's low levels of progress to their inherent group characteristics or the inadequacies of their family backgrounds. It lies in the process of young children learning about the structured categories described in Chapter 9. The categories serve a number of conceptual purposes:

- they have rich inductive potential – one can induce from the category characteristics of other members of the category;
- they capture properties that are difficult to see (such as inherited capabilities and special processes underlying psychological properties);

- they can be treated as though they have essences – there is an underlying reality or true nature that these categories reveal.

At-risk categories

So when a category such as "disadvantaged children" or "at-risk children" is developed, it comes with a set of features to order and has explanatory power. Difficulties in teaching and learning can be seen as examples confirming the category. In addition, teachers holding such beliefs can have a sense that their own lack of effectiveness can be attributed to the underlying properties and the essence of being this type of child.

How beliefs about teaching and learning influence expectations

Beliefs about how learning occurs, and where difficulties in learning and teaching are located, come from what Olson and Bruner have called folk pedagogies. Some of these general beliefs provide particularly strong rationales for ideas about deficiency, deprivation, and disadvantage, especially when they are used to explain a lack of effectiveness in an instructional programme. For example, as we noted in Chapter 1, beliefs that literacy development can be described as a single sequence of stages, provide a simple rationale for children being advanced or retarded relative to one normative line of progress. Beliefs that literacy is solely, or even primarily, constructed by children as they draw on information in their environment can be used to justify ideas that children are the problem, or their environments are, because they provide poor resources for constructing literacy knowledge.[2]

This book is based on the view that children construct their ideas about and ways of using written language from the everyday practices in which they participate and are observers. All children are inherently set to internalise and reinvent these ideas and ways, as they co-construct literacy development with significant family and community members within the channels offered by everyday practices. They develop multiple ways of using written language because what they know and what they become able to do is a reflection (and to some degree a replica) of their socialisation.

Locating sources of difficulties

High expectations held by teachers are derived from beliefs that effective patterns of co-construction can be achieved in their classrooms and schools. The corollary of this claim is that difficulties in developing conventional literacy at school are a reflection of the patterns of co-construction in classrooms. The source of the difficulties can be found, in large part, in curricular conditions and classroom activities. Admittedly, many of the difficulties may be attributable to how effectively the classroom activities connect with or incorporate what happens outside of school. But in this book we argue that this is something that is solvable through the classroom.[3]

The roles of apprenticeship and explicit teaching

The psychological processes involved in teachers' developing these beliefs are not dissimilar to the experiences of apprenticeship and explicit instruction that operate for children's co-construction of literacy. Being immersed in a community of teachers provides an apprenticeship-style basis for the development of ideas about learning and teaching. But general ideas about the nature of teaching and learning can be influenced by explicit teaching, particularly during one's initial teacher training. In this book, we argue that such teaching can influence a teacher to examine activities as a source of obstacles to effectiveness, rather than locating them in children alone.

Influence from the top

Explicit teaching can occur on the job. This is where the role of the principal can be clearly shown to have an impact on the effectiveness of schools. Studies of high-achieving schools serving poorer communities have shown that the schools' principals have explicitly fostered a collective set of beliefs about where effectiveness (or ineffectiveness) is located, and expectations about learning. In one study, the principals were described as having:

> ... *accepted no excuses regarding student achievement. They believed that it was the responsibility of the teacher, the principal and the school to do whatever was necessary to help all students succeed. They would not tolerate any conversation about parents being at fault for the child's situation. They felt it was the job of the school to succeed with the support of parents, but that it was*

not acceptable to say that the school couldn't do its job until parents did certain things. It was their view that the school gets the resources, the school has the teachers, so it's the school's responsibility to succeed with the child. (Sparks, 2001, page 59)

A less restricted vision

It is perhaps obvious that if you expect not to see much, you usually limit your view. In one school (the one from which the example of children's lack of knowledge about crayons came), fifty percent of the children were, by year three, one-and-a-half to two years below national norms in conventional literacy. In a professional development project there, the teachers tested their beliefs that the children were largely deficient in literacy skills at entry to school. They developed a checklist of "essential skills", such as concepts about print and being able to follow instructions. In fact, even on this highly prescriptive list of concepts and behaviours of school literacy, the children knew and could do much more than the teachers had assumed. The results of the project led them to conclude that, in general, the children actually brought with them "a very sound basis for learning".

Awareness of efficacy

The second element that contributes to high expectations is a teacher's own sense of effectiveness. Over twenty years ago, researchers first identified how teachers differ in the degree to which they believe that they can affect how well students can learn, even children who may be difficult to teach. From that time, studies have consistently demonstrated a statistically significant relationship between a teacher's strong sense of personal efficacy and the academic achievement of students from diverse cultural and language backgrounds.[4]

The sense of personal efficacy

A belief in one's own effectiveness depends on the context of teaching and can vary across different subject matter, showing that it is tied up with awareness of what one can do as a teacher. Teachers with a strong sense of efficacy are more open to new ideas and more willing to experiment with new methods to meet the needs of students, and they tend to have greater levels of planning and organisation. They have greater persistence and resilience and make greater efforts in the face of difficulties. The differences between teachers who have a strong sense of efficacy and those who do not can be seen in such day-to-day activities and interactions as making positive responses to children's errors and using grouping effectively for instruction. Teachers with a poor sense of efficacy favour a custodial orientation, relying on extrinsic inducements and sanctions to keep students on task. Teachers with a strong sense of efficacy support the development of children's intrinsic interests and developing independence.

The sense of collective efficacy

In addition to this sense of personal efficacy, there is a school community's collective sense of efficacy. Schools where teachers discuss difficulties in teaching children as seemingly insurmountable have been shown to have a low collective sense of efficacy that undermines teachers' sense of personal effectiveness. The corollary of this is that sharing beliefs about solving teaching problems supports personal efficacy. This is an important aspect of a school's "climate" – one that has been shown to influence achievement, irrespective of the backgrounds of children.

Reversing the cycle of inefficacy

Albert Bandura (1995) describes a depressing cycle in which a sense of unsolvable problems lowers beliefs in personal effectiveness, which in turn results in reduced commitment to teaching and innovating. The resulting impact on students further reduces the sense of being effective. We can see another example of the Matthew effects here, similar to those that affect children's progress. Bandura also describes the antidote – a collective sense of high-level efficacy in a school community at the beginning of an academic year predicts a school's academic achievement at the end of the year. This can be demonstrated even when the different characteristics of the children, their prior levels of achievement, and the staff's levels of experience are taken into account

The role of social influences in a sense of efficacy

Current models of the development of teachers' personal sense of efficacy show several major social influences on the process. These include experience of mastery as well as immersion in an effective community of learners. The most powerful influence is the experience of being effective. There are conditions to this, of course, such as whether the effectiveness is due to one's own actions or has been brought about with substantial help from elsewhere. But, for teachers, feedback from actual teaching experiences is critical – just as, for children, learning from performance during the actual reading and writing of texts is vital in developing effective literacy skills.

The picture of classrooms that we get from this is one of an ascending spiral of effectiveness – being effective reinforces a sense of efficacy that, in turn, feeds into innovation and the development of more effective instruction. In the absence of such experience, the reverse spiral of ineffectiveness can result.

Knowing about effectiveness

A third element found in teachers who have high expectations of their students is that, in addition to knowing that they *can* be effective, they know whether they *are* being effective. That knowledge is derived from specific information that these teachers have about teaching, learning, and achievement. An impressive feature of the school principals described earlier who rejected any rationales given for ineffectiveness being beyond the school's control was their knowledge about their students. They were able to tell an enquirer, for example, the reading level of every child in their schools (Sparks, 2001). This knowledge comes from gathering and having access to information that describes effectiveness. But it also comes from understanding what is, in fact, good evidence for effectiveness.

Good evidence for effectiveness

Good evidence describes the range of accomplishments that are important in learning to read and write. In the case of instruction in the first years of school, this means detailed information about the development of item knowledge, such as concepts about print and letter and sound relationships, as well as levels of accuracy and comprehension in reading and writing texts.

Acceptable and believable benchmarks

Good evidence can be related to acceptable and believable benchmarks. With children from diverse cultural and language backgrounds, there is a further challenge here. Is it appropriate to compare these children with children from communities of the majority cultural groups, especially soon after the beginning of instruction? After all, there are other issues to be taken into account at this stage; for example, the children's bilingual development and the appropriateness of children's language for the language of instruction (if it is a majority language, such as English).

This question is about what happens in development – a question that is both open and empirical. The weight of evidence reported throughout this book is that waiting for "readiness" and delaying instruction, or filling the curriculum with developmental experience rather than systematic literacy instruction, do not mean that children "catch up" with normal progress levels. In one study, which we look at in detail below, the view was taken that if children whose family language was other than English were provided with effective literacy instruction, they could acquire the language that they needed in the course of carrying out the literacy activities. Moreover, effective literacy instruction could accelerate their exposure to new vocabulary, thus creating reciprocal influences between literacy and language uses.

Being concerned about the disadvantages of unfair comparisons might result in denying children the high standards and effective instruction that they desperately need. We have argued similarly elsewhere for a parallel situation – that children who need to "catch up" should not be denied access to and use of the richest available texts for reading and writing.[5]

Using the evidence – a case study

A study of New Zealand urban schools serving Māori and Pacific Islands children in economically poor communities offers us an example of knowing how to select good evidence and how to use it. The study involved an intervention based on the professional development of teachers of year one children.[6] It started with collecting, for each school, a "broad band" of literacy measures of children after a year at school. The band included measures of item knowledge, validated for development in New Zealand schools, as well as measures of progress in text reading levels and writing. The risk analysis table shown in Chapter 4 represents this range.

Examining discrepancies in achievement

The teachers in these schools were already collecting information on individual children both during and at the end of the first year of instruction. Assessments such as running records were carried out for diagnostic purposes and for identifying children for Reading Recovery. But, generally, the teachers had not used the data to look systematically at the actual and expected progress of individuals or cohorts. Where this had been done, and marked discrepancies with national benchmarks had been found, the discrepancies were explained as illustrating the deficiencies of the children or their communities.

Discussion around explanations for these discrepancies formed the basis of the first professional development sessions. As reported in Chapter 4, the patterns of results across measures showed that, generally, the children had acquired the expected levels in letter knowledge and knowledge of sound and letter relationships by the end of the first year of school. Nevertheless, large discrepancies with national benchmarks for reading and writing of texts were apparent. However, having this information had not resulted in the schools focusing on enhancing instruction in these skills.

The professional development continued, using as a basis the information provided by the patterns and levels of achievement, for both individuals and cohorts. Most importantly, these same measures were used to check the effectiveness of the intervention. The risk analysis was then redone. It showed that major reductions in the levels of risk had been achieved by the seventy-seven teachers in the twelve schools.

Knowledge about effectiveness needs to be at a personal as well as a collective level. But, at both levels, the knowledge is useful only if it is based on good evidence that relates to important indices of progress across the range of learning that children need. Schools, as well as individual teachers, need mechanisms for collecting and collating this good evidence.

Final word

This book has been about how teachers can create the meeting of minds that Bruner says lies at the heart of effective teaching and learning. Understanding this problem requires a theoretical framework that places teachers, learners, and their shared understandings in classroom activities at its heart. Armed with this framework, two general approaches have been explored. Wide curricula with versatile activities in dynamic classroom communities are needed for both of these approaches to work.

The approaches have been described as strategies that enable children's emerging expertise to be incorporated into classroom activitiesand strategies that build children's awareness in those activities. These are not recipes. They come from the expertise that teachers develop, based on their own extensive knowledge, their critical awareness, and their high expectations.

The intention in writing this book was to provide sufficient examples and evidence for readers to understand the psychological processes involved in achieving a meeting of minds so that we can teach children with diverse language and cultural backgrounds more effectively.

End Notes

1   See, for example, the website www.schoolchange.ciera.org.
2   See Dyson (1999), Hemphill and Snow (1996), and McNaughton (1995) for further discussion of this point.
3   This is solvable for the conventional literacy valued by schools as well as for the new literacies that need to be valued by schools (New England Group, 1996).
4   This summary of teacher efficacy research is based on recent reviews from Tschannen-Moran, Woolfolk, Hoy, and Hoy (1998) and Bandura (1995).
5   See Chapter 6 and studies of schools and assessment issues by Timperley, Robinson, and Bullard (1999).
6   The project is reported in Phillips, McNaughton, and MacDonald (2001), and the theoretical basis for the professional development is described further in Chapter 9.

References

Adams, M. J. (2001). "Alphabetic Anxiety and Explicit, Systematic Phonics Instruction: A Cognitive Science Perspective". In S. B. Neuman and D. K. Dickinson (eds), *Handbook of Early Literacy Research*. New York: The Guilford Press, pp. 66–80.

Allington, R. L. and Woodside-Jones, H. (1999). "The Politics of Literacy Teaching: How 'Research' Shaped Educational Policy". *Educational Researcher* vol 28 no. 8, pp. 4–13.

Ashton-Warner, S. (1966). *Teacher*. Hammondsworth: Penguin Books.

Au, K. H. (1993). *Literacy Instruction in Multicultural Settings*. New York: Harcourt Brace.

Au, K. H. and Maaka, M. J. (1998). "Ka Lama O Ke Kaiaulu: Research on Teacher Education in a Hawaiian community". *Pacific Educational Research Journal*, vol. 9 no.1, pp. 65–85.

Baker, L. (1996). "Social Influences on Metacognitive Development in Reading". In C. Cornoldi and J. Oakhill (eds), *Comprehension Difficulties: Processes and Interventions*. Mahwah, NJ: Lawrence Erlbaum, pp. 331–352.

Bandura, A. (1995). "Exercise of Personal and Collective Efficacy in Changing Societies". In A. Bandura (ed), *Self-Efficacy in Changing Societies*. Cambridge: Cambridge University Press, pp. 1–45.

Bartolome, L. I. (1998). *The Misteaching of Academic Discourses: The Politics of Language in the Classroom*. Boulder: Westview Press.

Betsinger, A. M., Garcia, S. B., and Guerra, P. L. (2001). "Up for Scrutiny". *Journal of Staff Development*, vol. 22 no.2, pp. 24–27.

Biemiller, A. (1999). *Language and Reading Success*. Cambridge, MA: Brookline Books.

Blackmore, S. (1999). *The Meme Machine*. New York: Oxford University Press.

Bransford, J. D., Brown, A. L., and Cocking, R. R. (eds), (1999). *How People Learn: Brain, Mind, Experience and Schools*. Washington D.C.: National Academy Press.

Bransford, J. D. and Schwartz, D. L. (1999). "Rethinking Transfer: A Simple Proposal with Multiple Implications". In A. Iran-Nejad and P. D. Pearson (eds), *Review of Research in Education 24*. Washington D.C.: American Educational Research Association, pp. 61–100.

Bronfenbrenner, U. (1979). *The Ecology of Human Development*. Cambridge, MA: Harvard University Press.

Brown, A. L. (1994). "The Advancement of Learning". *Educational Researcher*, vol. 23 no. 8, pp. 4–12.

Brown, A. L. (1997). "Transforming Schools into Communities of Thinking and Learning about Serious Matters". *American Psychologist*, vol. 52 no. 4, pp. 399–413.

Brown, A. L. and Campione, J. C. (1994). "Guided Discovery in a Community of Learners". In K. McGilly (ed), *Classroom Lessons: Integrating Cognitive Theory and Classroom Practice*. Cambridge, MA: The MIT Press, pp. 229–272.

Bruner, J. S. (1980). *Beyond the Information Given*. London: Allen and Unwin.

Bruner, J. S. (1996). *Culture and Education*. Cambridge, MA: Harvard University Press.

Bull, A. F. (1996). "Expository Writing Patterns of African American Students". *English Journal*, January, pp. 27–36.

Bus, A. G. (2001). "Joint Caregiver-Child Storybook Reading: A Route to Literacy Development". In S. B. Neuman and D. K. Dickinson (eds), *Handbook of Early Literacy Research*. New York: The Guilford Press, pp. 179–191.

Bussis, A. M. (1982). "Burn it at the Casket: Research, Reading, Instruction and Children's Learning of the First R". *Phi Delta Kappan 64*, pp. 237–241.

Camps, A. and Milian, M. (eds), (2000). *Metalinguistic Activity in Learning to Write.* Amsterdam: Amsterdam Press.

Cazden, C. (1988). *Classroom Discourse.* Portsmouth, NH: Heinemann.

Cazden, C. (1993). "Immersing, Revealing and Telling: A Continuum from Implicit to Explicit Teaching". Paper presented to the Second International Conference on Teacher Education in Second Language Teaching, City Polytechnic of Hong Kong.

Chang-Wells, G. L. and Wells, G. (1993). "Dynamics of Discourse: Literacy and the Construction of Knowledge". In E. A. Forman, N. Minick and C. A. Stone (eds), *Contexts for Learning: Sociocultural Dynamics in Children's Development.* New York: Oxford University Press, pp. 58–90.

Clanche, P. (1999). "New Caledonia: *Coutume* and Culture in Education". *International Review of Education*, vol. 45 no. 3 and no. 4, pp. 359–365.

Clay, M. M. (1985). "Engaging with the School System". *New Zealand Journal of Educational Studies 20*, pp. 20–38.

Clay, M. M. (1991). *Becoming Literate: The Construction of Inner Control.* Auckland: Heinemann Education.

Clay, M. M. (1993). *An Observation Survey of Early Literacy Achievement.* Auckland: Heinemann Education.

Clay, M. M. (1998). *By Different Pathways to Common Outcomes.* York, ME: Stenhouse Publishers.

Clay, M. M. and Cazden, C. B. (1990). "A Vygotskian Interpretation of Reading Recovery". In L. C. Moll (ed), *Vygotsky and Education: Instructional Implications and Applications of Socio-Historical Psychology.* Cambridge, MA: Cambridge University Press pp. 206–222.

Cochran-Smith, M. and Lytle, S. L. (1999). "Relationship of Knowledge and Practice: Teacher Learning in Communities". In A. Iran-Nejad and P. D. Pearson (eds), *Review of Research in Education 24.* Washington D.C.: American Educational Research Association, pp. 249–306.

Cordova, D. I. and Leeper, M. R. (1996). "Intrinsic Motivation and the Process of Learning: Beneficial Effects of Contextualizing, Personalization, and Choice". *Journal of Educational Psychology 88*, pp. 715–730.

Cummins, J. (1986). "Empowering Minority Students: A Framework for Intervention". *Harvard Educational Review 56*, pp. 18–36.

Dahl, K. L., Scharer, P. L., Lawson, L. L., and Grogan, P. R. (1999). "Phonics Instruction and Student Achievement in Whole Language First Grade Classrooms". *Reading Research Quarterly*, vol. 34 no 3, pp. 312–341.

Darling-Hammond, L. (1997). *The Right to Learn: A Blueprint for Creating Schools That Work.* San Francisco: Jossey-Bass.

Darling-Hammond, L. (1998). "Teachers and Teaching: Testing Policy Hypotheses from a National Commission Report". *Educational Researcher*, vol. 27 no. 1, pp. 5–15.

Delpit, L. (1995). *Other People's Children: Cultural Conflict in the Classroom.* New York: The New Press.

Department of Education (1985). *Reading in Junior Classes.* Wellington: School Publications.

Detterman, D. K. and Sternberg, R. J. (eds), (1993). *Transfer on Trial: Intelligence, Cognition, and Instruction.* Norwood, NJ: Ablex.

Dickinson, D. K. (2001a). "Book Reading in Preschool Classrooms: Is Recommended Practice Common?". In D. K. Dickinson and P. O. Tabors (eds), *Beginning Literacy and Language: Young Children Learning at Home and School.* Baltimore: Paul Brookes Publishing, pp. 175–201.

Dickinson, D. K. (2001b). "Putting the Pieces Together: Impact of Preschool on Children's Language and Literacy Development in Kindergarten". In D. K. Dickinson and P. O. Tabors (eds), *Beginning Literacy and Language: Young Children Learning at Home and School.* Baltimore: Paul Brookes Publishing, pp. 257–288.

Dickinson, D. K. and Smith, M. W. (1994). "Long-Term Effects of Preschool Teachers' Book Readings on Low-Income Children's Vocabulary and Story Comprehension". *Reading Research Quarterly,* vol. 29 no. 2, pp. 104–122.

Dickinson, D. K. and Sprague, K. E. (2001). "The Nature and Impact of Early Childhood Care Environments on the Language and Early Literacy Development of Children from Low Income Families". In S. B. Neuman and D. K. Dickinson (eds), *Handbook of Early Literacy Research.* New York: The Guilford Press. pp. 263–280.

Dickinson, D. and Tabors, P. O. (2001). *Beginning Literacy with Language: Young Children Learning at Home and at School.* Baltimore: Paul Brookes Publishing.

Duthie, C. (1994). "Nonfiction: A Genre Study for the Primary Classroom". *Language Arts,* vol. 71 no. 8, pp. 585–595.

Dyson, A. H. (1997). *Writing Superheroes: Contemporary childhood, popular culture, and classroom literacy.* New York: Teachers College Press.

Dyson, A. H. (1999a). "Transforming Transfer: Unruly Children, Contrary Texts and the Persistence of the Pedagogical Order". In A. Iran-Nejad and P. D. Pearson (eds), *Review of Research in Education 24.* WashingtonD.C.: American Educational Research Association, pp. 141–172.

Dyson, A. H. (1999b). "Writing (Dallas) Cowboys: A Dialogic Perspective on the 'What did I write?' Question". In J. S. Gaffney & B. J. Askew (eds), *Stirring the Waters: A Tribute to Marie Clay.* Portsmouth NH: Heinemann, pp. 127–147.

Dyson, A. H. (2001). "Writing and Children's Symbolic Repertoires: Development Unhinged". In S. B. Neuman and D. K. Dickinson (eds), *Handbook of Early Literacy Research.* New York: The Guilford Press, pp 126–141.

Elley, W. B. (1989). "Vocabulary Acquisition from Listening to Stories". *Reading Research Quarterly,* vol. 24 no. 2, pp. 174–186.

Elley, W. B. (1992). *How in the World Do Children Read?* New York: The International Association for the Evaluation of Educational Achievement.

Elster, C. (1994). "Patterns within Preschoolers' Emergent Readings". *Reading Research Quarterly,* vol. 29 no. 4, pp. 403–417.

Emmett, M., Pollock, J., and Limbrick, L. (1996). *An Introduction to Language and Learning.* Melbourne: Oxford University Press.

Feldman, C. F. and Kalmar, D. A. (1996). "Some Educational Implications of Genre-Based Mental Models: The Interpretive Cognition of Text Understanding". In D. R. Olson and N. Torrance (eds), *The Handbook of Education and Human Development.* Oxford: Blackwell, pp. 433–460.

Fisher, D., Lapp, D., and Flood, J. (1999). "How is Phonics Really Taught?". In T. Shanahan and F. V. Rodriguez-Brown (eds), *National Reading Conference Yearbook 48,* pp. 134–145.

Flockton, L. and Crooks, T. (1997). *Reading and speaking assessment results 1996. (National Education Monitoring Report 6).* Wellington: Ministry of Education.

Flockton, L. and Crooks, T. (1999). *Writing assessment results 1998 (National Education Monitoring Report 12).* Wellington: Ministry of Education.

Flockton, L. and Crooks, T. (2000). *Assessment Results for Māori Students 1999. (National Education Monitoring Report 13).* Wellington: Ministry of Education.

Foorman, B. R., Francis, D. J., Fletcher, J. M., Schatschneider, C., and Mehta, P. (1998). "The Role of Instruction in Learning to Read: Preventing Reading Failure in At-Risk Children". *Journal of Educational Psychology*, vol. 90 no. 21, pp. 37–55.

Forman, E. A., Minick, N., and Stone, C. A. (eds), (1993). *Contexts for Learning: Sociocultural Dynamics in Children's Development*. New York: Oxford University Press.

Foster, M. (1995). "African American Teachers and Culturally Relevant Pedagogy". In J. A. Banks and C. A. McGee Banks (eds), *Handbook of Research on Multicultural Education*. New York: McMillan, pp. 570–581.

Freedman, A. (1994). "'Do As I Say': The Relationship between Teaching and Learning New Genres". In A. Freedman and P. Medway (eds), *Genre and the New Rhetoric*. Bristol, PA: Taylor and Francis, pp. 191–210.

Fukkink, R. G. and de Glopper, K. (1998). "Effects of Instruction in Deriving Word Meaning from Context: A meta analysis". *Review of Educational Research*, vol. 68 no. 4, pp. 450–469.

Fullan, M. (2001). *Leading in a Culture of Change*. San Francisco: Jossey-Bass.

Gardner, H. (1991). *To Open Minds*. New York. Basic Books.

Gee, J. P. (1998). "Foreword". In L. I. Bartolome, (1998). *The Misteaching of Academic Discourses: The Politics of Language in the Classroom*. Boulder: Westview Press.

Gelman, S. A., Coley, J. D., Rosengren, K. S., Hartman, E., and Pappas, A. (1998). "Beyond Labelling: The Role of Maternal Input in the Acquisition of Richly Structured Categories". *Monographs of the Society for Research in Child Development*, vol. 63 no. 1.

Gilmore, A. (1998). *School Entry Assessment: The First National Picture*. Wellington: Ministry of Education.

Gilmore, A., Croft, C., and Reid, N. (1981). *BURT Word Reading Test: New Zealand Revision*. Wellington: New Zealand Council for Educational Research.

Glasswell, K. (1999). *The Patterning of Difference: Teachers and Children Constructing Development in Writing*. Unpublished doctoral dissertation, University of Auckland, New Zealand.

Glasswell, K., McNaughton, S., and Parr, J. (1993). "Teachers' Expectations of Children's Knowledge about Writing on Entry to J1". Paper presented at the New Zealand Association for Research in Education Annual Conference, Hamilton, December 2–5, 1993.

Glasswell, K., Parr, J., and McNaughton, S. (2001). "Working with William: Teaching, Learning and the Joint Construction of a Poor Writer". Unpublished. Queensland University of Technology, Australia.

Glynn, T., Berryman, M., Atvars, K., and Harawira, W. (1997). *Hei Awhina Matua: A Home and School Behavioural Programme*. Final report to the Research Section of the New Zealand Ministry of Education. Wellington: Ministry of Education.

Goldenberg, C. (2001). "Making Schools Work for Low-Income Families in the 21st Century". In S. B. Neuman and D. K. Dickinson (eds), *Handbook of Early Literacy Research*. New York: The Guilford Press, pp. 211–231.

Gombert, J. E. (1992). *Metalinguistic Development*. New York: Harvester Wheatsheaf.

Goodman, Y. (1990). *How Children Construct Literacy*. Newark: International Reading Association.

Goodnow, J. J. and Collins, W. A. (1990). *Development According to Parents: The Nature, Sources and Consequences of Parents' Ideas*. Hillsdale, NJ: Lawrence Erlbaum.

Goodridge, M. J. (1995). "Activity Systems for Writing: A Co-constructivist Analysis of Children's Emergent Writing Development at Home and in the Transition to School in

Three Diverse Sociocultural Settings". Unpublished PhD thesis. University of Auckland, New Zealand.

Goswami, U. (2001). "Early Phonological Development and the Acquisition of Literacy". In S. B. Neuman and D. K. Dickinson (eds), *Handbook of Early Literacy Research*. New York: The Guilford Press, pp. 111–125.

Guthrie, J. T. and Wigfield, A. (eds), (1999). "Special Issue: How Motivation Fits into a Science of Reading". *Scientific Studies of Reading*, vol. 3 no.3, pp. 199–281.

Gutierrez, K. D. (1992). "A Comparison of Instructional Contexts in Writing Process Classrooms with Latino Children". *Education and Urban Society*, vol. 24 no. 2, pp. 244–262.

Hart, B. and Risley, T. R. (1980). "In Vivo Language Intervention: Unanticipated General Effects". *Journal of Applied Behavior Analysis, 13*, pp. 407–432.

Hart, B. and Risley, T.R. (1995). *Meaningful Differences in the Everyday Experience of Young American Children*. Baltimore: Paul Brookes Publishing Co.

Hartman, D. K. (1995). "Eight Readers Reading: The Intertextual Links of Proficient Readers Reading Multiple Passages". *Reading Research Quarterly*, vol. 30 no. 3, pp. 520–561.

Hattie, J. (1999). "Influences on Student Learning". Unpublished paper. Inaugural lecture, University of Auckland, New Zealand.

Heath, S. B. (1983). *Ways with Words: Language, Life, and Work in Communities and Classrooms*. Cambridge: Cambridge University Press.

Hemphill, L. and Snow, C. (1996). "Language and Literacy Development: Discontinuities and Differences". In D. R. Olson and N. Torrance (eds), *The Handbook of Education and Human Development*. Oxford: Blackwell, pp. 173–201.

Hiebert, E. H. and Martin, L. A. (2001). "The Texts of Beginning Reading Instruction." In S. B. Neuman and D. K. Dickinson (eds), *Handbook of Early Literacy Research*. New York: The Guilford Press, pp. 361–376.

Hoffman, J. V., McCarthy, S. J., Abbott, J., Christian, C., Corman, L., Curry, C., Dressman, M., Elliott, B., Matherne, D., and Stahle, D. (1994). "So What's New in the New Basals? A Focus on First Grade". *Journal of Reading Behavior, 26*, pp. 47–73.

Juel, C. (1994). *Learning to Read and Write in One Elementary School*. New York: Springer-Verlag.

Kame'enui, E. J. and Carnine, D. W. (1998). *Effective Teaching Strategies that Accommodate Diverse Learners*. NJ: Merrill.

Karmiloff-Smith, A. (1992). *Beyond Modularity: A Developmental Perspective on Cognitive Science*. Cambridge, MA: MIT Press.

Knapp, M. S., Sheilds, P. M., and Turnbull, B. J. (1995). "Academic Challenge in High-Poverty Classrooms". *Phi Delta Kappan*, vol. 76 no. 10, pp. 770–780.

Ladson-Billings, G. (1992). "Reading Between the Lines and Beyond the Pages: A Culturally Relevant Approach to Literacy Teaching". *Theory into Practice*, vol. 31 no. 4, pp. 312–320.

Ladson-Billings, G. (1994). *The Dream Keepers: Successful Teachers of African American Children*. San Francisco: Jossey Bass.

Landauer, T. K. (1998). "Learning and Representing Verbal Meaning: The Latent Semantic Analysis Theory". *Current Directions in Psychological Science*, vol. 7 no. 5, pp. 161–164.

Lave, J. and Wenger, E. (1991). *Situated Learning: Legitimate Peripheral Participation*. Cambridge: Cambridge University Press.

Learning Media (1998). *School Entry Assessment: A Guide for Teachers*. Wellington: Learning Media.

Lee, C. D. (2000). "Signifying in the Zone of Proximal Development". In C. D. Lee and P. Smagorinsky (eds.), *Vygotskian Perspectives on Literacy research: Constructing Meaning Through Collaborative Inquiry*, Cambridge: Cambridge University Press. pp.191 – 225.

Lee, C. D. and Medenball, R. (2001). "'The Blacker the Berry the Sweeter the Juice' revisited: African American Vernacular English as a Resource for Narrative Writing and Instructional Design". Paper presented at *The American Educational Research Association Annual Meeting*, Seattle, Washington, April 4–10, 2001.

Literacy Experts Group. (1999). *Report of the Literacy Experts Group to the Secretary of Education*. Wellington: Ministry of Education.

Literacy Task Force (1999). *Report of the Literacy Task Force*. Wellington: Ministry of Education.

Losey, K. M. (1995). "Mexican American Students and Classroom Interaction: An Overview and Critique". *Review of Educational Research*, vol. 65 no. 3, pp. 283–318.

Luke, A. and Luke, C. (2001). "Adolescence Lost/Childhood Regained: On Early Intervention and the Emergence of the Techno-Subject". *Journal of Early Childhood Literacy*, vol.1 no.1, pp. 91–120.

MacIntyre, E. and Freppon, P. A. (1994). "A Comparison of Children's Development of Alphabetic Knowledge in a Skills-Based and Whole Language Classroom". *Research in the Teaching of English*, vol. 28 no. 4, pp. 381–417.

McLachlan, S. (1996). "The Power of Visual Language: Māori in Illustration in Beginning Reading Instruction". Unpublished MA thesis, University of Auckland, New Zealand.

McNaughton, S. (1987). *Being Skilled: The Socialisations of Learning to Read*. London: Methuen.

McNaughton, S. (1995). *Patterns of Emergent Literacy: Processes of Development and Transition*. Auckland: Oxford University Press.

McNaughton, S. (1996). "Ways of Parenting and Cultural Identity". *Culture and Pscyhology*, vol. 2 no. 2, pp. 173–201.

McNaughton, S. (1997). "Being a Teacher and Having a Curriculum". *English in Aotearoa*, *31*, pp. 5–11.

McNaughton, S. (1999a). "Developmental Diversity and Beginning Literacy Instruction at School". In J. S. Gaffney & B. J. Askew (eds), *Stirring the Waters: The Influence of Marie Clay*. Portsmouth, NH: Heinemann, pp.3–16.

McNaughton, S. (1999b). "Do New Zealand Teachers Teach Phonics? How Would We Know?". *Reading Forum NZ, 3*, pp. 28–35.

McNaughton, S.(2001). "A Beneficial Influence? Learning and Teaching in Native Schools". In J. Simon and L. T. Smith (eds), *A Civilising Mission? Perceptions and Representations of the New Zealand Native Schools System*. Auckland: Auckland University Press, pp. 89–139.

McNaughton, S., Phillips, G., and MacDonald, S. (2000). "Curriculum Channels and Literacy Developments over the First Year of Instruction". *New Zealand Journal of Educational Studies*, vol. 35 no.1, pp.49–59.

Martens, P., Flurkey, A., Meyer, R., and Udell, R. (1999). "Inventing Literacy Identities: Intratextual, Intertextual, and Intercontextual Influences on Emerging Literacy". In T. Shanahan and F. Rodriguez-Brown (eds), *Ninety-Ninth Yearbook of the National Reading Reading Conference*, pp. 73–85.

Ministry of Education (1994). *English in the New Zealand Curriculum*. Wellington: Learning Media.

Moll, L. C. (1999). "Writing and Communication: Creating Strategic Learning Environments for Students". In E. R. Hollins and E. I. Oliver (eds), *Pathways to Success in School: Culturally Responsive Teaching*. Mahwah, NJ: Lawrence Erlbaum, pp. 73–84.

Nash, R. (1993). *Succeeding Generations: Family Resources and Access to Education in New Zealand.* Auckland: Oxford University Press.

Nicholson, T. (1992). "Historical and Current Perspectives on Reading". In C. J. Gordon, G. D. Labercane, and W. R. McEackern (eds), *Elementary Reading: Process and Practice.* Needham Heights, MA: Ginn.

Nicholson, T. (1997). "Closing the Gap on Reading Failure: Social Background, Phonemic Awareness, and Learning to Read". In B. A. Blachman (ed), *Foundations of Reading Acquisition and Dyslexia. Implications for Early Intervention.* Mahwah, NJ: Lawrence Erlbaum, pp. 381–407.

Nicholson, T. and Gallienne, G. (1995). "Struggletown Meets Middletown: A Survey of Reading Achievement Levels among 13-year-old Pupils in Two Contrasting Socioeconomic areas". *New Zealand Journal of Educational Studies*, vol. 30 no. 1, pp. 15–23.

Neuman, S. B. (1999). "Books Make a Difference: A Study of Access to Literacy". *Reading Research Quarterly*, vol. 34 no.3, pp. 286–311.

Ogbu, J. U. (1991). "Cultural Mode, Identity and Literacy". In J. W. Stigler, R. A. Shweder, and G. Herdt (eds), *Cultural Psychology: Essays on Comparative Human Development.* Cambridge: Cambridge University Press.

Olson, D.R. and Bruner, J.S. (1996). "Folk Psychology and Folk Pedagogy". In D.R. Olson and N. Torrance (eds), *The Handbook of Education and Human Development: New Models of Learning, Teaching and Schooling.* Oxford: Blackwell Publishers, pp. 9–27.

Olson, D. R. and Torrance, N. (eds), (1996). *The Handbook of Education and Human Development: New Models of Learning, Teaching and Schooling.* Oxford: Blackwell Publishers.

Palincsar, A. S., Brown, A.L., and Campione, J. (1993). "First Grade Dialogues for Knowledge Acquisition and Use". In E. A. Forman, N. Minick, and C. A. Stone (eds), *Contexts for Learning: Sociocultural Dynamics in Children's Development.* New York: Oxford University Press, pp. 43–57.

Pappas, C. C. and Zecler, L. B. (eds), (2001). *Transforming Literacy Curriculum Genres: Working with Teacher Researchers in Urban Classrooms.* Mahwah, NJ: Lawrence Erlbaum.

Paratore, J. R. (1995). "Implementing an Intergenerational Literacy Project: Lessons Learned". In L. M. Morrow (ed) *Family Literacy: Connections in Schools and Communities.* International Reading Association.

Paratore, J. R., Hindin, A., Krol-Sinclair, B., Duran, P., Emig, J., and McClure, K. (2000). "Improving Parent-Teacher Communication through Family Literacy Portfolios". Paper presented at the World Congress of Reading, Auckland, New Zealand.

Patthey-Chavez, G. G. and Goldenberg, C. (1993). *Changing Instructional Discourse for Changing Students: The Instructional Conversation.* In R. Macias and R. Garcia Ramos (eds), *Changing Schools for Changing Students: An Anthology of Research on Language Minorities, Schools and Society.* Santa Barbara, CA: University of California Linguistic Minority Research Institute, pp. 205-230.

Pelligrini, A. and Galda, L. (1998). *The Development of School-based Literacy: A Social Ecological Perspective.* London: Routledge.

Perkins, F. D. (1999). "'People Like Us': African American Children Respond to Self-Affirming Texts". In E. R. Hollins and E. I. Oliver (eds), *Pathways to Success in School: Culturally Responsive Teaching.* Mahwah NJ: Lawrence Erlbaum, pp 47–60.

Phillips, G. E. (1997). *An Analysis of the Co-construction of Context in Beginning Reading Instruction.* Unpublished doctoral dissertation. University of Auckland, New Zealand.

Phillips, G., McNaughton, S., and MacDonald, S. (2001). "Picking up the Pace: Effective Literacy for Accelerated Progress over the Transition into Decile 1 Schools". *Report to the Ministry of Education*. Wellington: Ministry of Education.

Phillips, L. M., Norris, S. P., and Mason, J. M. (1996). "Longitudinal Effects of Early Literacy Concepts on Reading Achievement: A Kindergarten Intervention and Five-Year Follow-Up". *Journal of Literacy Research, 28*, pp. 173–195.

Pinker, S. (1999). *Words and Rules*. London: Weidenfeld and Nicholson.

Pressley, M. (1998). *Reading Instruction That Works: The Case for Balanced Teaching*. New York: The Guilford Press.

Pressley, M., Allington, R., Wharton-McDonald, R., Block, C. C., and Morrow, L. M. (2001). *Learning to Read: Lessons from Exemplary First-Grade Classrooms*. New York: The Guilford Press.

Pressley, M., Rankin, J., and Yokoi, L. (1996). "A Survey of Instructional Practices of Primary Teachers Nominated as Effective in Promoting Literacy". *The Elementary School Journal*, vol. 96 no. 4, pp. 363–384.

Reutzel, D. R., Hollingsworth, P. M., and Eldredge, J. L. (1994). "Oral Reading Instruction: The Impact on Student Reading Development". *Reading Research Quarterly*, vol. 29 no. 1, pp. 40–65.

Robbins, C. and Ehri, L. C. V. (1994). "Reading Storybooks to Kindergarteners Helps Them Learn New Vocabulary Words". *Journal of Educational Psychology*, vol. 86 no.1, pp. 54–64.

Rogoff, B. (1990). *Apprenticeship in Thinking: Cognitive Development in Social Context*. Oxford: Oxford University Press.

Rogoff, B., Matusov, E., and White, C. (1996). "Models of Teaching and Learning: Participation in a Community of Learners". In D. R. Olson and N. Torrance (eds), *The Handbook of Education and Human Development: New Models of Learning, Teaching and Schooling*. Oxford: Blackwell Publishers, pp. 388–414.

Rogoff, B., Bartlett, L., and Turkanis, C. G. (2001). "Lessons about Learning as a Community". In B. Rogoff, C. G. Turkanis, and L. Bartlett (eds), *Learning Together: Children and Adults in a School Community*. Oxford: Oxford University Press.

Rosenhouse, J., Feitelson, D., Kita, B., and Goldstein, Z. (1997). "Interactive Reading Aloud to Israeli First Graders: Its Contribution to Literacy Development. *Reading Research Quarterly*, vol. 32 no. 2, pp. 168–83.

Rothbaum, F., Pott, M., Azuma, H., Miyake, K., and Weisz, J. (2000). "The Development of Close Relationships in Japan and the United States: Paths of Symbiotic Harmony and Generative Tension". *Child Development*, vol.7 no. 5, pp. 1121–1476.

Saunders, W., Goldenberg, C., and Hamman, J. (1992). "Instructional Conversations Beget Instructional Conversations". *Teaching and Teacher Education*, vol. 8 no. 22, pp. 199–218.

Schieffelin, B. B. and Ochs, E. (1986). *Language Socialisation across Cultures*. Cambridge: Cambridge University Press.

Siegler, R. S. (2000). "The Rebirth of Children's Learning". *Child Development*, vol. 71 no. 1, pp. 26–35.

Simon, J. and Smith, L. T., (eds), (2001). *A Civilising Misssion? Perceptions and Representations of the New Zealand Native Schools System*. Auckland: Auckland University Press.

Skinner, D., Bryant, D., Coffman, J., and Campbell, F. (1998). "Creating Risk and Promise: Children's and Teachers' Co-constructions in the Cultural World of Kindergarten". *The Elementary School Journal*, vol. 98 no. 4, pp. 297–311.

Slavin, R. E. and Madden, N. A. (eds), (2001). *Success for All: Research and Reform in Elementary Education*. Mahwah, NJ: Lawrence Erlbaum.

Smith, J. and Elley, W. (1994). *Learning to Read in New Zealand*. Auckland: Longman.

Smith, J. and Elley, W. (1997). *How Children Learn to Write*. Auckland: Longman.

Snow, C. E., Barnes, W., Chandler, J., Goodman, I., and Hemphill, L. (1991). *Unfulfilled Expectations: Home and School Influences on Literacy*. Cambridge, MA: Harvard University Press.

Snow, C. E., Burns, S., and Griffin, P. (eds), (1998). *Preventing Reading Difficulties in Young Children*. Washington D.C.: National Academy Press.

Sparks, D. (2001). "Follow the Winners: Educators Bring Top Reading Strategies to Struggling Schools". *Journal of Staff Development*, vol. 22 no. 2, pp. 58–60.

Stanovich, K. E. (1986). "Matthew Effects in Reading: Some Consequences of Individual Differences in the Acquisition of Literacy". *Reading Research Quarterly*, vol. 21 no. 4, pp. 360–401.

Stanovich, K. E., West, R. F., Cunningham, A. E., Cipielewski, J., and Siddiqui, S. (1996). "The Role of Inadequate Print Exposure as a Determinant of Reading Comprehension Problems". In C. Cornoldi and J. Oakhill (eds), *Reading Comprehension Difficulties: Processes and Intervention*. Mahwah, NJ: Lawrence Erlbaum, pp. 15–32.

Stanovich, K. E., Cunningham, A. E., and West, R.F. (1998). "Literacy Experiences and the Shaping of Cognition". In S. G. Paris and H. M. Wellman (eds), *Global Prospects for Education: Development, Culture and Schooling*. Washington D.C.: American Psychological Association, pp. 253–288.

Sternberg, R. J. (1998). "Abilities are Forms of Developing Expertise". *Educational Researcher*, vol. 27 no.3, pp. 11–21.

Sulzby, E. (1994). "Children's Emergent Reading of Favourite Storybooks: A Developmental Study". In R. B. Ruddell, M. R. Ruddell, and H. Singer (eds), *Theoretical Models and Processes in Reading*, Fourth Edition. Newark, DE: International Reading Association, pp. 244–280.

Swanborn, M. S. L. and de Glopper, K. (1999). "Incidental Word Learning while Reading: A Meta-Analysis". *Review of Educational Research*, vol. 69 no. 3, pp. 261–285.

Taylor, B. M., Anderson, R. C., Au, K. H., and Raphael, T. E. (2000). "Discretion in the Translation of Research into Policy: A Case from Beginning Reading". *Educational Research*, vol 29 no. 6, pp.16–26.

Tharp, R. G. and Gallimore, R. (1988). *Rousing Minds to Life: Teaching, Learning, and Schooling in Social Context*. Cambridge, MA: Cambridge University Press.

Thelen, E. (1995). "Motor Development: A New Synthesis". *American Psychologist*, vol. 50 no. 2, pp.79–95.

Timperley, H., Robinson, V. M. J., and Bullard, T. (1999). *Strengthening Education in Mangere and Otara Evaluation: First Evaluation Report*. Wellington: Ministry of Education.

Trumbull, E., Rothstein-Fiskh, C. and Greenfield, P. M. (2001). "Ours and Mine: Cultural Views of Collectivism and Individualism Come into Play in School Behavior". *Journal of Staff Development*, vol. 22 no. 2.

Tschannen-Moran, M., Hoy, A. W., and Hoy, W. K. (1988). "Teacher Efficacy; Its Meaning and Measure". *Review of Educational Research*, vol. 68 no. 2, pp. 202–248.

Tunmer, W. E. and Chapman, J. W. (1997). "An Investigation of Language-Related and Cognitive-Motivational Factors in Beginning Reading Instruction". *Final Report to the Ministry of Education*. Massey University: Educational Research and Development Centre.

Tunmer, W. E., Chapman, J. W., Ryan, H. A., and Prochnow, J. E. (1998). "The Importance of Providing Beginning Readers with Explicit Training in Phonological Processing Skills". *Australian Journal of Learning Disabilities*, vol. 3 no.2, pp. 4–14.

Turoa, L., Wolfgramm, E., Tanielu, L., and McNaughton, S.M. (2002). "Pathways Over the Transition to School: Studies in Family Literacy Practices and Effective Classroom Contexts for Māori and Pacifika Children". *Final Report to the Ministry of Education*. Wellington: Ministry of Education.

Valsiner, J. (1987). *Culture and the Development of Children's Action*. Chichester: Wiley.

Valsiner, J. (1988). "Ontogeny of Co-construction of Culture within Socially Organised Environmental Settings". In J. Valsiner, (ed), *Child Development within Culturally Structured Environments*, Volume Two. NJ: Ablex.

Vygotsky, L. S. (1978). *Mind in Society: the Development of Higher Psychological Processes*. M. Cole, V. John-Steiner, S. Scribner, and E. Souberman, eds and trans. Cambridge, MS: Harvard University Press.

Wagemaker, H. (1992). "Preliminary Findings of the IEA Literacy Study: New Zealand Achievement in the National and International Context". *Educational Psychology 12*, no. 3 and no. 4, pp. 195–214.

Wenger, E. (1998). *Communities of Practice: Learning, Meaning and Identity*. Cambridge: Cambridge University Press.

White, E. B. (1952). *Charlotte's Web*. UK: Hamish Hamilton.

Whitehurst, G. J. and Lonigan, C. J. (1998). "Child Development and Emergent literacy". *Child Development*, vol. 69 no. 3, pp. 848–872.

Whitehurst, G. J. and Lonigan, C. J. (2001). "Emergent Literacy: Development from Prereaders to Readers". In S. B. Neuman and D. K. Dickinson (eds), *Handbook of Early Literacy Research*. New York: The Guilford Press, pp. 11–29.

Wilkinson, I. A. G. (1998). "Dealing with Diversity: Achievement Gaps in Reading Literacy among New Zealand Students". *Reading Research Quarterly*, vol. 33 no. 2, pp. 144–167.

Wilkinson, I. A. G. and Townsend, M. (2000). "From Rata to Rimu: Grouping for Instruction in Best Practice New Zealand Classrooms". *Reading Teacher*, vol. 53 no. 6, pp. 460–471.

Wood, D. (1998). *How Children Think and Learn*. Second Edition. Oxford: Blackwell.

Wylie, C., Thompson, J., and Lythe, C. (1999). *Competent Children at Eight: Families, Early Education, and Schools*. Wellington: New Zealand Council for Educational Research.

Yuill, N. (1996). "A Funny Thing Happened on the Way to the Classroom: Jokes, Riddles and Metalinguistic Awareness in Understanding and Improving Poor Comprehension in Children". In C. Cornoldi and J. Oakhill (eds), *Reading Comprehension Difficulties: Processes and Intervention*. Mahwah NJ: Lawrence Erlbaum, pp. 193–220.

Index

A

ability grouping, 110–111
activities, 23–25, 27, 112
    authentic and meaningful, 127–128
    community of learners, 127–128
    familiar, *see* familiar activities
    family literacy, *see* home activities
    home, *see* home activities
    learning identities, 126–127, 129
    teaching acts, *see* teaching acts
    versatile, *see* versatile activities
    see also curricula
African American students, 72–73
    Black English, 62, 69
    effective teachers, *see* effective teaching
    enhancing awareness, 78, 186–187
    explicit or direct commands, 68–70
    local texts and illustrations, 59–60, 63, 65
    narratives, 108
    personalisation, 68, 115
    writing process, 92–93
alphabetic knowledge, 89, 91
alternative schools, 16–17
Americans,
    African, *see* African American students
    European, 108
apprenticeship process, 29–30, 133, 143, 209
'at' principle, 26, 30–31
    what is the teacher trying to get at?, 19–20
    where are the children at?, 18–19
at-risk children, 15–17, 157, 208
    alternative kinds of schools, 16
    effective teachers, 16
    new horizons, 16–17
    phonics, *see* phonics
    risk,
        definitions, 17, 18
            at risk because of children's deficiency, 17
            risky business of school, 14, 18, 20, 93, 136, 151
        not being at expected levels, 82, 84, 214
    solution: in the ordinary classroom, 17
Au, Katherine, 28, 62, 71–72
audience feedback, 149–150
authenticity, 127–129, 143, 193
"author's chair", 60
"author's theatre", 60–61

B

balance,
    explicit teaching, 179–180
    phonics, *see* phonics
    reading comprehension, 177–179
    requirements for, 51, 76, 148
    see also incorporation

"balance of rights", 68, 157
Bandura, Albert, 211
Bartolome, 30
basal reader series, 77, 132
beginning instruction, *see* literacy
being an expert, *see* expert awareness
bilingualism, 65, 147, 148, 188, 213
bill of rights, 136–137, 142–143, 151, 180
Black English, 62, 69, 108
black students, *see* African American students
Blackmore, Susan, 151
book floods, 146–147
books, *see* reading; texts
Brice Heath, Shirley, 78, 155–156
Brown, Ann, 129–130, 154, 196–197
Bruner, Jerome, 8–9, 18–19, 30, 48, 99, 208, 215
building on the familiar, *see* incorporation

C

Campione, 129
caregiver talk, 189
categories, 189, 207–208
    see also at-risk children
Cazden, 48, 108
Chang-Wells, 124
children,
    at-risk, *see* at-risk children
    older, *see* older children
Clanche, Pierre, 70
classroom activities, 25, 43, 126, 215
    authentic and meaningful, 128
    classroom language, *see* classroom language
    effectiveness, 209
    versatile activities, *see* versatile activities
classroom diversity, *see* diversity
classroom language, 8–9, 122–123, 142, 147, 186
    community of learners, 176
    contextualisation, 123–124
        types of context, 124–125
            experiencing rules for language contexts, 125
    novice and, 122
        language that children need, 122–123
    requirements, 187
    shared discourse, 130
    teacher's talk, 192
classroom learning, 107
    classroom language, *see* classroom language
    learning identities, 126–127
classroom texts, 57
    engaging familiarity of texts, 64
    familiar content, *see* familiar content
    familiar illustrations, *see* familiar illustrations
    familiar language, 61–62

Index

Notes